"Boersma invites us to consider the relationship between theology and biblical studies by taking us on a tour of the inner workings of his discipline. He helps us understand how theology views the Bible as a witness to all things being reconciled in our Lord Jesus Christ, a book saturated in metaphysical presuppositions, governed by the providence of God, which we interpret as his church, in anticipation of our final end: the contemplation of God. This book and its companion are must-reads for those pursuing theological or biblical studies—a clear and winsome invitation to step beyond artificial but strongly held divisions in seminaries and universities today."

Adam Johnson, associate professor of theology, Torrey Honors Institute at Biola University

"I was trained in a method of biblical scholarship that insisted that as long as one employed the methodologies of historical-critical scrutiny of the Bible, one could arrive at the determinate meaning of the biblical text. But what if the overriding property of the Bible is that the risen Christ elects to speak through these texts? Hans Boersma here explores how that fundamental theological conviction makes all the difference. His case is largely convincing to this biblical scholar, and I hope it will be widely considered among my colleagues in the biblical studies guild."

Wesley Hill, associate professor of New Testament at Western Theological Seminary, Holland, Michigan

"I am blessed to have been trained in institutions and by people who decried any sharp divisions between biblical studies and theology, yet I respected the distinct contributions of both. Boersma's book gives words to this sentiment. Each chapter reminds biblical scholars of broad commitments they likely share, but ones their discipline makes easy to ignore. Boersma grounds a call to increased appreciation and common mission in the aim of all theology, namely respecting the sacramental character of Scripture and its role in pointing all who hear it to the worship of God."

Amy Peeler, associate professor of New Testament at Wheaton College and Graduate School

"With apologies to Shakespeare, we have to admit the impediments to the marriage of true minds before we can reconcile them. Communication lies at the heart of healthy relationships, and Boersma does a good job of sharing what's on his theological mind to his biblical scholar counterpart. My prayer is that this exchange will lead not to another battle for the Bible (Why do the theological disciplines rage?) but, rather, to a closer working relationship between biblical scholars and theologians. For exegesis and theology are joined at the hip, and a dislocated hip only cripples the body of Christ."

Kevin J. Vanhoozer, research professor of systematic theology at Trinity Evangelical Divinity School

"In this slim but rich volume, Hans Boersma invites us to consider Christ as not just the climax of the biblical story but the starting point and goal of our engagement with the Bible. He beautifully reminds us that we engage with the Scriptures to find Christ and to be drawn further into the love of God in Christ. Provocatively suggesting that our efforts to elevate the Bible often end up devaluing it, he challenges us to wrestle with many notions that we today take for granted. While a quick read, the questions he raises and the theological vision he casts for our biblical engagement will long stay with you."

Kristin Deede Johnson, dean and vice president of academic affairs, professor of theology and Christian formation, Western Theological Seminary

"This book is useful and exhilarating! Hans Boersma takes us on a tour of those 'elements that help us to read Scripture . . . as a sacrament'—Christology, (Platonic) metaphysics, providence, church, and heaven. His insistence on the mystagogical telos of Scripture, coupled with a penetrating critique of today's common exegetical methods, retrieves patristic approaches (Irenaeus, Athanasius, Origen, Augustine, and many others) that are still devalued today. Here exploration and polemic are conjoined, so some may want to engage the author vigorously in, for example, his exuberant claims for Christian Platonism, or his insistence that entry into the divine life is contemplative rather than active in nature. Finally Boersma commends to our minds and hearts the image of full-blooded scriptural exegesis as 'an exploration of an enchanted forest that holds ever deeper mysteries' when we maintain Scripture's 'proper penultimacy' to life in Christ."

Edith M. Humphrey, William F. Orr Professor Emerita of New Testament, Pittsburgh Theological Seminary

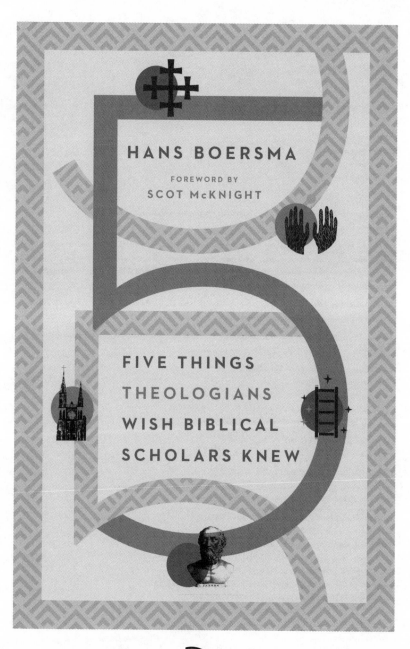

HANS BOERSMA

FOREWORD BY
SCOT McKNIGHT

FIVE THINGS
THEOLOGIANS
WISH BIBLICAL
SCHOLARS KNEW

ivp
Academic
An imprint of InterVarsity Press
Downers Grove, Illinois

220.6

InterVarsity Press
P.O. Box 1400, Downers Grove, IL 60515-1426
ivpress.com
email@ivpress.com

InterVarsity Press® is the book-publishing division of InterVarsity Christian Fellowship/USA®, a movement of
students and faculty active on campus at hundreds of universities, colleges, and schools of nursing in the United States
of America, and a member movement of the International Fellowship of Evangelical Students. For information about
local and regional activities, visit intervarsity.org.

Scripture quotations, unless otherwise noted, are from The Holy Bible, English Standard Version, copyright © 2001 by
Crossway Bibles, a division of Good News Publishers. Used by permission. All rights reserved.

The publisher cannot verify the accuracy or functionality of website URLs used in this book beyond the date of
publication.

Cover design and image composite: David Fassett
Interior design: Jeanna Wiggins
Images: Gothic church illustration: © Catarina Bessell / Getty Images
       art deco texture: © supermimicry / iStock / Getty Images Plus
       Plato: © ZU_09 / DigitalVision Vectors / Getty Images

ISBN 978-0-8308-5390-8 (print)
ISBN 978-0-8308-5391-5 (digital)

Printed in the United States of America ♾

InterVarsity Press is committed to ecological stewardship and to the conservation of natural resources in all our
operations. This book was printed using sustainably sourced paper.

Library of Congress Cataloging-in-Publication Data
Names: Boersma, Hans, 1961- author.
Title: Five things theologians wish biblical scholars knew / Hans Boersma.
Description: Downers Grove, IL : IVP Academic, [2021] | Includes
  bibliographical references and index.
Identifiers: LCCN 2021013302 (print) | LCCN 2021013303 (ebook) | ISBN
  9780830853908 (paperback) | ISBN 9780830853915 (ebook)
Subjects: LCSH: Bible—Criticism, interpretation, etc. | Theology.
Classification: LCC BS511.3 .B6525 2021 (print) | LCC BS511.3 (ebook) |
  DDC 220.6—dc23
LC record available at https://lccn.loc.gov/2021013302
LC ebook record available at https://lccn.loc.gov/2021013303

P 25 24 23 22 21 20 19 18 17 16 15 14 13 12 11 10 9 8 7 6 5 4 3 2 1

Y 42 41 40 39 38 37 36 35 34 33 32 31 30 29 28 27 26 25 24 23 22 21

To John, Lucia, Gabriel, and Zoe

Kathryn, Gerald, Theodore, Timothy, and Titus

Macrina

Johannes, Abigail, and Jude

May our Lord Jesus himself

interpret to you in all the Scriptures

the things concerning himself.

CONTENTS

DETAILED CONTENTS

FOREWORD

Scot McKnight

THEOLOGY, HANS BOERSMA REMINDS US, never stands still. Sometimes, however, it goes downhill. It is the responsibility of biblical theologians to remind those on the downhill that there's a better path. A confession is in order, however: theology itself routinely checkmates my exegetical instructions and reminds me that the orthodox gospel summons me to stay in line or I, too, will be on the downhill. Not that Boersma is on the downhill. No, not at all. What needs to be emphasized is the mutual responsibility theologians and biblical exegetes have for one another.

In the last two decades or so something has arisen that is called the *theological interpretation of Scripture*, that reading the Bible isn't simply about authorial intention in historical context with methods plied in all directions. Any reading of the history of interpreting the Bible reveals generational shifts in what one might call the meaning of the text in its context. The very term *context*, of course, has shifted at times from one's own theological history to the ancient Near East or the Greco-Roman world or Judaism as we can now know it. Very well then. Boersma's theology is at work in advocating for a kind of theological, christological reading of Scripture in a sacramental sense.

Even then one might press into play the question, Which theology? Whose theology? Is it Catholic, Orthodox, Reformed, Lutheran, creedal/Platonic, creedal/non-Platonic, Pentecostal, Stone-Campbell, dispensational, Anglican, or Episcopalian? I found his definition particularly clarifying:

> The primary task of theology (and let's forget here about the distinction between biblical and dogmatic theology) is not to explain the historical meaning of the text but to use the Scriptures as a means of grace in drawing the reader to Jesus Christ. In other words, biblical interpretation is not a historical discipline. To use a patristic expression, it is *mystagogical* in character: biblical interpretation leads the reader into the mystery of God in Christ. The theologian's terminus does not lie in the history behind the text or even in the text itself. The theologian attends to Scripture as a sacramental means of entering into the mystery of God. Theology (and Scripture as a means) aims at nothing less than the divine life itself.[1]

That's a big ask for someone who has devoted his life to studying the Bible in its context. I might suggest here that one needs to distinguish "task of theology" from the "terminus" of theology because for me one is required first to listen to the voice of the text so that the voice can, like Dante, be our guide to that beatific vision. A text cannot be sacramental until that text first speaks. And, if I may, does a mystagogical aim of the text listen to the visions of that heaven well enough, to texts such as Revelation, where we encounter a new Jerusalem where a beatific vision is not so clear as a vibrant city shapes our vision? Is his vision of heaven too heavenly? I ask myself.

Boersma's robust claims will sustain many returning to the question, What is theology? I like the question and I don't think biblical theologians ponder it often enough. I was on the Greek island of Rhodes

---

[1]From the introduction, 5-6.

with my wife, Kris, where I combined vacation and exploration with morning reading and writing. During that time, I read Hans Boersma's *Scripture as Real Presence*. I was mesmerized by his method and claims, I was curious what it all meant, and I worried what would become of the method I use in New Testament studies. I wrote to Hans to tell him I appreciated his book and asked him whether he thought the apostle Paul's reading of the Old Testament was "sacramental." He wrote back from his sabbatical location, the Netherlands, and said he thought so and described Paul's approach to be "Christ-filled." Hans was of course right about Paul's hermeneutic being Christ-filled (I was reading Richard Hays at the same time), and this sets the tone for our two books. The historical-critical method, which is nothing other than being a historian, whatever its values (and they are many), is not how Jesus or the apostles read their Bibles, it is not how the patristics or medievals read their Bibles, and it is not how the Reformers read their Bibles. It is in fact an Enlightenment method. That is all I need to say here: if we want to comprehend the gospel of the Christ of the Bible, we will need at least to reconsider these our good predecessors' hermeneutics.

I like much of what I read in this book. Boersma makes us think again of what Scripture study is all about. Our purpose in exegesis, because we are Christians in love with God, cannot be contained by historical intention and must be re-formed into knowledge of God, of others, and of all creation. The core teaching of Jesus, after all, was that we are to love God and to love others as ourselves (Mk 12:28-34). Scripture reading must fit in that bed. Revelation has a personal telos and an origin: we encounter God in the face of Christ.

> Christians, therefore, are not (at least, not in an ultimate sense) people of the book. The book, while indispensable and properly venerated as a sacrament of the Word, is not itself God's final revelation: only Christ is. Because Christ is sacramentally present in the Scriptures—even in the wisdom literature and the historical narratives of the Old Testament—we turn to the

Scriptures as a means to God's final revelation in Christ. God assumes flesh in Christ, so that Christ truly is the Word incarnate. Yes, Scripture too makes God present—incarnation and inscripturation are closely analogous. But Scripture is not the Word of God itself. The eternal Logos hypostatically (personally) identifies himself with human nature, not with a book. A single-minded emphasis on authorial intent shifts the focus from Scripture's spiritual telos to its historical point of origin. In doing so, it runs the real risk of bibliolatry: the substitution of a book for God in Christ.[2]

Christ is the point, but there is in the Bible not just that singular focus on a person but a theology of history unfolding the gospel. Is perhaps the gospel the Bible's center? I say that only because I believe the gospel itself is an announcement that the story of Israel has come to its fulfillment in Jesus Christ as Israel's Messiah. The Christ of Christian theology is a Jewish Messiah, and a Jewish Messiah makes sense only in a narrative that takes us from longing to completion. We did not get our Bible and then, by studying it, derive the gospel on the basis of inductive exegesis and conclusion. Rather, the gospel itself—this narrative story fulfilled in Christ—gave rise to the Scriptures as those texts that witnessed to that gospel and its Christ. In the beginning was the gospel, not the Scriptures. The gospel that created the Scriptures as what best represented that gospel became the formative shape of the Nicene Creed's second article, the heart of the creed. Creed, then, is not something other than gospel but a rearticulation of the gospel itself, and it centers on the story of Jesus.

Who is the second article of the creed, the one about Jesus the Jewish Messiah now dressed up in new clothes for a new day, what Boersma calls Platonism. The chapter "No Plato, No Scripture," which

[2]From the introduction, 8-9.

is more about the realism of a Christian Platonism and a disavowal of nominalism, is the critical moment in Boersma's thesis. Not a few of us will be nervous with the claims he makes about Platonism. His interest here is an ontology that has at least some roots in the Jewish Shema from Deuteronomy 6 and Paul's own reshaping of that ontology in 1 Corinthians 8:6, where Paul finds both the Father and the Son in the Shema itself. I can live with an ontology that owes its roots to this kind of material interpretation by the apostle Paul as he refashions the central Jewish creed. But, what about a Hebrew cosmology? A Judean cosmology? A Jewish-Christian cosmology? *Homoousios* may have Platonic undertones, but one God, a messiah story, and an atonement from sin by sacrifice of the God-man is hardly Platonic.

Perhaps he will say it is, and at that point I will stand up, go to my shelves, pull off some Plato, and begin reading. One of the hazards of being a biblical theologian, at least for some of us, is not permitting folks like Plato and Aristotle into our discussions. Should we?

ACKNOWLEDGMENTS

THE IDEA FOR THIS BOOK WASN'T MY OWN. David McNutt of IVP
Academic first came to me with the idea of two complementary books,
one written by a theologian and one by a biblical scholar. Even the
titles of the two books are his rather than mine. Needless to say, I am
thankful for the trust David and IVP Academic have placed in me, and
it is an honor to engage in this project together with Scot McKnight,
author of this book's companion volume. I hope that the end result—
both Scot's book and my own—is what David had in mind.

Upon David's suggestion for a book on "five things theologians wish
biblical scholars knew," I first approached twenty-seven colleagues and
students, asking them what their personal list of five items would look
like. Rather than mention every one of them by name, let me just offer
a collective thank you. Although the responses obviously varied, a
number of common themes emerged, which informed the structure
(as well as the contents) of the book. Thank you all for helping me
think through the often-difficult interpretive issues involved!

I first presented chapters one, three, and five as the Thomas C.
Oden Patristics Lectures at Trinity School for Ministry in January
2020. I am grateful to Joel Scandrett, the director of the Robert E.
Webber Center, for inviting me to deliver the lecture series, as well as
to Wesley Hill, David Ney, and Bill Witt for their generous and

thoughtful engagement with my talks. I also want to thank the students and the entire TSM community for their hospitality and for the stimulating theological discussion.

It was a real privilege to use a draft of the book for a course on theological interpretation at Nashotah House Theological Seminary in Wisconsin. It is most encouraging to note the strong interest in sacramental interpretation among the students of "the House." I loved teaching the course, and I owe the students a big thank you for engaging the topic with such enthusiasm and seriousness. It is deeply gratifying to note the impact that Gar Anderson's visionary leadership is making on Nashotah House, both in numbers and in spirit. May our good Lord continue to make us thrive as a faithful instrument in his kingdom.

I owe a special word of thanks to friends and family members who read the whole book: Gar Anderson, Ryan Brandt, Micah Hogan, Blythe Kingcroft, Corine Milad, and Nomi Pritz-Bennett; as well as to Inter-Varsity Press's anonymous peer reviewer. Their numerous suggestions have greatly improved the book, and I hope that you'll forgive my stubbornness in occasionally sticking with the original idea or wording. I am especially grateful to my wife, Linda, not just because she read the manuscript in its entirety but especially because her unwavering love is a constant reminder to me of the ultimate aim of biblical interpretation.

ABBREVIATIONS

ACW   Ancient Christian Writers

ANF   *The Ante-Nicene Fathers.* Edited by Alexander Roberts and James Donaldson. 1885–1887. 10 vols. Reprint, Peabody, MA: Hendrickson, 1994

BDB   Francis Brown, S. R. Driver, and Charles A. Briggs, *Hebrew and English Lexicon*

BMW   The Bible in the Modern World

DR   *The Downside Review*

DTIB   *Dictionary for Theological Interpretation of the Bible.* Edited by Kevin J. Vanhoozer. Grand Rapids, MI: Baker Academic, 2005

FC   Fathers of the Church

IJPS   *International Journal of Philosophical Studies*

IJST   *International Journal of Systematic Theology*

JTI   *Journal of Theological Interpretation*

LCC   Library of Christian Classics

LNTS   Library of New Testament Studies

MST   Mediaeval Sources in Translation

NPNF   *Nicene and Post-Nicene Fathers of the Christian Church.* Edited by Philip Schaff. 14 vols. Reprint, Peabody, MA: Hendrickson, 1994

PL   Patrologia Latina. Edited by J.-P. Migne. 162 vols. Paris,
          1857–1886

Princ.   Origen, *De Principiis* (*On First Principles*)

ProEccl   *Pro Ecclesia*

PTS   Patristische Texte und Studien

SJT   *Scottish Journal of Theology*

SP   *Studia Patristica*

SVSPCS   St. Vladimir's Seminary Press Classics Series

TEG   Traditio Exegetica Graeca

VC   *Vigiliae Christianae*

VCSup   Supplements to Vigiliae Christianae

VE   *Vox Evangelica*

WBC   Word Biblical Commentary

WSA   *The Works of Saint Augustine: A Translation for the Twenty-
          First Century*

INTRODUCTION

BIBLICAL AND DOGMATIC THEOLOGY

Neither this book's title nor its implied topic should be taken too seriously. Talk about the relationship between theologians and biblical scholars assumes the existence of two distinct academic disciplines—even more, it extends this division from the disciplines to the people embarking on them: apparently, some scholars engage in dogmatic (or systematic) theology while others are biblical scholars. Both presuppositions are terribly wrong.

With this opening salvo I don't mean to take a swipe at the editors of IVP Academic. David McNutt is an excellent editor, and his suggestion that I write a book titled *Five Things Theologians Wish Biblical Scholars Knew* had my immediate and warm support. After all, though I may be convinced that the disciplinary boundary between biblical studies and doctrinal reflection is illegitimate, this boundary does exist in practice. And current academic trends worsen the situation. The drift is toward ever-shorter programs of seminary and other theological training, which allow for fewer and fewer opportunities for biblical and doctrinal students to take courses in each other's disciplines. As a result, it is increasingly common for students to obtain a PhD in biblical studies without ever having seriously engaged in dogmatic theology and vice versa. By publishing two books, one by a biblical scholar and one by a theologian, IVP Academic is doing its part to bring the two disciplines closer together (or, as I hope, to render the very distinction obsolete).

The division between biblical and dogmatic theology goes back at least to 1787, when Johann P. Gabler delivered an inaugural address at the University of Altdorf titled *De justo discrimine theologiae biblicae et dogmaticae regundisque recte utriusque finibus* ("On the Proper Distinction Between Biblical and Dogmatic Theology and the Specific Objectives of Each").[1] Whatever we may think of the distinction between biblical and dogmatic theology, the reality is that since then seminaries and theological departments have almost universally adopted the distinction.

Gabler sharply delineated biblical theology, defined as the historical study of positive sources (Scripture), and dogmatic theology, which he thought of as the speculative or philosophical engagement of religious truths. Explaining this distinction, he writes: "There is truly a *biblical theology*, of historical origin, conveying what the holy writers felt about divine matters; on the other hand there is a *dogmatic theology* . . . of didactic origin, teaching what each theologian philosophises rationally about divine things, according to the measure of his ability or of the times, age, place, sect, school, and other similar factors."[2] Gabler, deeply shaped by Enlightenment thought, maintained that biblical theology was grounded in historical criticism. Biblical theology's task was one of historical reconstruction, followed

---

[1]For an English translation and commentary, see John Sandys-Wunsch and Laurence Eldredge, "J. P. Gabler and the Distinction Between Biblical and Dogmatic Theology: Translation, Commentary, and Discussion of His Originality," *SJT* 33 (1980): 133-58.

[2]Gabler in Sandys-Wunsch and Eldredge, "J. P. Gabler," 137; emphasis added.

by the dogmatic attempt of ferreting out the theological themes that continued to be of significance.

Dogmatic theology was, for Gabler, a second step, one that takes account not just of the theology found in the Bible but also of the various demands of one's own historical context. As John Sandys-Wunsch and Laurence Eldredge put it: "Gabler saw the particular need of his period to be for a dogmatic theology that was in agreement with reason, clearly expressed, and aware of the new human wisdom especially in philosophy and history."[3] Gabler explained that the multiplicity of theological traditions and dogmatic developments could be explained by the fact that these were not grounded in biblical theology alone.

Two things stand out in Gabler's account. First, biblical theology is a purely historical discipline. And second, dogmatic theology is strictly a second step. Gabler's procedure neatly divided the two disciplines, and this has served to render much of the subsequent history of biblical theology impervious to ecclesial and dogmatic concerns. To be sure, not all biblical theology proceeds along the lines of Gabler's inaugural lecture. Many biblical scholars, especially those of a more conservative bent, question the legitimacy and value of searching for the history behind the text. Grammatical-historical exegesis is much more firmly wedded to the text itself, and its practitioners typically don't share Gabler's skepticism vis-à-vis the miraculous or supernatural events that are recounted throughout the biblical narrative. Mostly, however, they do adopt Gabler's approach by working from the ground up, moving from positive (biblical) theology to speculative (dogmatic) theology.

For instance, in a much-quoted article, New Testament scholar D. A. Carson approvingly refers to a four-level interpretation approach as devised by Graham Cole:

---

[3]Sandys-Wunsch and Eldredge, "J. P. Gabler," 148.

At the first level, the Bible itself must be understood exegetically, within its literary and historical contexts, with appropriate attention devoted to literary genre, attempting to unfold authorial intent so far as it is disclosed in the text. At level 2, the text must be understood within the whole of biblical theology, including where it fits into and what it contributes to the unfolding storyline and its theology. At level 3, the theological structures found in the text are brought to bear upon, and understood in concert with, other major theological emphases derived from Scripture. At level 4, all teachings derived (or ostensibly derived) from the biblical text are subjected to and modified by a larger hermeneutical proposal (e.g., Trinitarian action, God's love and freedom, or something vague such as "what was disclosed in Jesus").[4]

I suspect that Cole and Carson see level one as engaging in a traditional form of grammatical-historical exegesis, with level two then placing the exegetical outcome within the broader theological trajectory of Scripture. (This second level is where much of the study of biblical themes of individual books—and of Scripture as a whole—typically occurs, something that has flourished greatly through the growth of biblical theology in the nineteenth and twentieth centuries.) Levels three and four are obviously more theological in character. It is here that other biblical themes (at level 3) and broader theological teachings (at level 4) enter into the picture. Carson observes that whereas traditional interpreters of Scripture operate mostly at levels one and two, recent advocates of the so-called theological interpretation of Scripture often operate mostly at levels three and four, sometimes at the cost of paying attention to levels one and two.

---

[4]D. A. Carson, "Theological Interpretation of Scripture: Yes, But . . . ," in *Theological Commentary: Evangelical Perspectives,* ed. R. Michael Allen (London: T&T Clark, 2011), 206-7.

I shouldn't run ahead of myself. In every chapter that follows, I propose an angle of reintegrating levels one and two with levels three and four, while simultaneously questioning the neat division of these levels in the first place. Let me simply observe here that Carson's brief summary of Cole's approach gives little indication of how Christology, metaphysics, providence, ecclesiology, and heavenly contemplation affect one's exegetical work. It is hard to avoid the conclusion that Carson and Cole—along with many other evangelical scholars— advocate an approach that treats theology as an afterthought. Indeed, if one takes Gabler's distinction seriously, it is easy to imagine dog- matic theology as simply disappearing from the scene, except perhaps in continuing to serve by way of a posteriori checks and balances, ensuring that one's interpretation of the biblical text isn't out of line with biblical teaching found elsewhere in Scripture. Why engage in dogmatic theology at all if biblical theology has already managed to establish the biblical-theological content apart from philosophical and doctrinal presuppositions?

THE OBJECT OF THEOLOGY

Now, I may actually be sympathetic to the abolition of dogmatic the- ology; that is to say, a dogmatic theology that accepts its consignment to the third and fourth stages of biblical engagement is simply not worth its salt. Inasmuch as Scripture has God himself for its subject matter, it is theological (that is to say, doctrinal or dogmatic) from the outset. The notion that we begin with trying to understand the text and subsequently arrive at theological or dogmatic conclusions fails to capture what the Bible is all about—and it also fails to understand what theologians are supposed to do. The primary task of theology (and let's forget here about the distinction between biblical and dog- matic theology) is not to explain the historical meaning of the text but to use the Scriptures as a means of grace in drawing the reader to Jesus Christ. In other words, biblical interpretation is not a historical discipline. To use a patristic expression, it is *mystagogical* in character: biblical interpretation leads the reader into the mystery of God in Christ. The theologian's terminus does not lie in the history behind the text or even in the text itself. The theologian attends to Scripture as a sacramental means of entering into the mystery of God. Theology (and Scripture as a means) aims at nothing less than the divine life itself.

The distinction I am alluding to here is reminiscent of the sharp debate between the Princetonians and the Mercersburg theologians in the mid-nineteenth century. This in-house Reformed debate pitched the Common Sense philosophy advocated by the Princeton school of Charles Hodge over against the idealist Romanticism of the Mercersburg theology of John W. Nevin and Philip Schaff. Common Sense philosophy was grounded in the empirical, Baconian tradition and as such adopted nominalist presuppositions, which William DiPuccio summarizes as follows: "(1) Only individual things are real. (2) Since every individual is unique, there can be no common nature or essence among them. Nominalism concludes, therefore, that (3) the common names used to designate groups of individuals according to similar attributes are merely subjective abstractions."[5] As DiPuccio explains, Hodge's Princetonian theology was grounded in the modern dualism between mind and matter and between God and world, a dualism that he inherited from Immanuel Kant and René Descartes.[6] As Nevin saw it, the propositionalism of the Princetonian tradition erred in identifying the object of faith with the propositions or teachings of Scripture rather than with Christ.[7]

In contrast to Hodge, the Mercersburg theologians took their starting point in Christian Platonism and, in line with this, in a realist

---

[5]William DiPuccio, *The Interior Sense of Scripture: The Sacred Hermeneutics of John W. Nevin*, Studies in American Biblical Hermeneutics 14 (Macon, GA: Mercer University Press, 1998), 11.
[6]DiPuccio, *Interior Sense of Scripture*, 9.
[7]DiPuccio, *Interior Sense of Scripture*, 13.

epistemology. For Nevin, this meant the following: "(1) Universal ideas are objective and ontological realities rather than creatures of the mind. (2) These ideas constitute the essence or nature of individuals and natural laws. (3) Universal ideas, therefore, are the foundation of all knowledge."[8] Nevin's acceptance of Christian Platonism rendered him sympathetic to the catholicity of the Great Tradition as well as to aspects of the Romanticism of Friedrich Schleiermacher and Samuel Taylor Coleridge.[9] As a result, Nevin and his Mercersburg colleagues worked with a participatory ontology: they regarded signs and reality as inwardly linked, so that they treated the language of Scripture as the sacramental means that links the believer directly to God in Christ as the object of faith.[10] For Nevin, explains DiPuccio, "the object of theology is neither speculation nor abstraction, but the realities themselves—that is, the ontic and the holy."[11] As Nevin saw it, the soul's capacity to behold God himself means that it is through intuition rather than induction that the soul has immediate communion with God.[12]

My project is in basic continuity with that of Nevin and the Mercersburg theologians. Both are deeply sympathetic to the patristic treatment of Scripture, which treats the Bible not as an end in itself but as a sacramental means of making God present to the church and to the individual believer.[13] Nevin's approach offered a basic reiteration of the sacramental hermeneutic that he found in the church

---

[8]DiPuccio, *Interior Sense of Scripture*, 10.
[9]Throughout this book, I speak of the Great Tradition as referring to the patristic and medieval tradition (East and West), which was grounded in a Christian Platonic (realist) metaphysic. Without in any way minimizing the numerous individual differences among theologians of the Great Tradition, it is nonetheless fair to distinguish it as a whole from Western modes of theologizing that originate in the late medieval and early modern nominalist turn in metaphysics.
[10]DiPuccio, *Interior Sense of Scripture*, 65-74.
[11]DiPuccio, *Interior Sense of Scripture*, 74.
[12]DiPuccio, *Interior Sense of Scripture*, 149.
[13]See my discussion of a sacramental hermeneutic in *Scripture as Real Presence: Sacramental Exegesis in the Early Church* (Grand Rapids, MI: Baker Academic, 2017).

fathers and the medieval tradition, and that has continued unabated in Eastern Orthodoxy and can be traced also in various strands of Catholic and Anglican thought. It is an approach that rejects a modern epistemology that begins with individual objects or events and that instead takes its starting point in eternal forms, christologically conceived as "located" within the eternal Logos. Put differently, it is the Christ-centered faith in eternal providence that motivated the Great Tradition to treat the biblical text as a sacramental means of grace drawing believers into the life of God rather than as a mere repository of historical and doctrinal truths.

Needless to say, Scripture does present a history of salvation, and it does make theological truth claims. The point, therefore, is not to downplay history or doctrinal truth. But what Nevin and others discovered is that Scripture in the Great Tradition never simply identifies the meaning of the text with authorial intent. Since the purpose of the biblical text is sacramental, it is only when, in faith, the believer has arrived at Christ himself that the Scripture truly yields its highest meaning. The reason, therefore, that the Great Tradition moved from history to spirit (or from the historical level to the allegorical, moral, and eschatological levels) in interpretation is that these earlier Christians recognized that meaning occurs in the encounter of faith between the believer and the sacramental reality to which Scripture points.

Christians, therefore, are not (at least, not in an ultimate sense) people of the book. The book, while indispensable and properly venerated as a sacrament of the Word, is not itself God's final revelation: only Christ is. Because Christ is sacramentally present in the Scriptures —even in the Wisdom literature and the historical narratives of the Old Testament—we turn to the Scriptures as a means to God's final revelation in Christ. God assumes flesh in Christ, so that Christ truly is the Word incarnate. Yes, Scripture too makes God present— incarnation and inscripturation are closely analogous. But Scripture is not the Word of God itself.[14] The eternal Logos hypostatically (personally) identifies himself with human nature, not with a book. A single-minded emphasis on authorial intent shifts the focus from Scripture's spiritual telos to its historical point of origin. In doing so, it runs the real risk of bibliolatry: the substitution of a book for God in Christ.

HOW TO UPHOLD SCRIPTURE:
A CHAPTER OVERVIEW

In no way do I mean to downplay the significance of Scripture. My concern is to reiterate that Scripture's ultimate meaning is not this-worldly but otherworldly. Scripture is not the sacramental reality (*res*) itself, but the indispensable outward means (*sacramentum*) that makes Christ present. We venerate Scripture, lifting it high in liturgical procession, but we worship God alone.

It is my conviction that only when we treat Scripture as sacramental rather than as an end in itself do we truly hold a high view of it. In a nominalist metaphysic, created things (including human words) are unhinged from their ideal, invisible realities. The result is that Scripture ends up being treated as a mere object, from which we attempt to wrest its original meaning by way of empirical research. For the purposes of finding meaning, such an objective or empirical

---

[14]For Joseph Cardinal Ratzinger, Scripture is a *witness* to revelation and should not be identified with it. Accordingly, he maintains, "You cannot put revelation in your pocket like a book you carry around with you." *God's Word: Scripture—Tradition—Office*, ed. P. Hünermann and T. Söding, trans. H. Taylor (San Francisco: Ignatius, 2008), 52. In response, the evangelical theologian Douglas A. Sweeney insists that Scripture actually *is* revelation, which "in this day and age, can be packaged, transported, and carried in our pockets." "Ratzinger on Scripture, Tradition, and Church: An Evangelical Assessment," in *Joseph Ratzinger and the Healing of the Reformation-Era Divisions*, ed. Emery de Gaál and Matthew Levering (Steubenville, OH: Emmaus Academic, 2019), 367-68. I would suggest that a way forward may be found here by treating Scripture as analogous with but not identical to the incarnation. Scripture sacramentally participates in divine revelation and makes it really present, but only Christ himself is the fullness of God's revelation. So, in an indirect sense Sweeney's statement may be allowed to stand. But (using Chalcedonian Christology) it is more fully the case that God suffered on the cross than that we hold divine revelation in our pocket, for God does not *assume* text in Scripture; he *assumes* flesh in Christ.

approach to Scripture *treats* it as a purely natural, purely human book—regardless of what our faith commitments about inspiration may tell us. In applying scientific methodology to the Bible, we devalue it: it becomes a mere object. Just like Baconian science tries to master the natural world, so Baconian interpretation tries to master the biblical text. The irony here is that precisely when we exalt the outward object (Scripture) as the be-all and end-all of our interpretive endeavor, our methodology treats it as an inert, lifeless object, which we have at our scholarly disposal. When we unhinge Scripture from the reality that gives it meaning we lose any and all spiritual significance.

I have purposely, therefore, used the term *Scripture* in each of the chapter titles. The exegetical efforts of biblical scholars are often motivated by a deep desire to do justice to Scripture as the Word of God. This desire animates many a search for the original meaning of the text. The underlying idea is that only when we subject ourselves as readers to what the text actually says (rather than impose our own subjective notions onto the text) do we retain its authority. I am genuinely sympathetic to this concern of much historical-biblical scholarship. Surely, we must eschew any arbitrary imposition of our subjective sentiments onto Holy Scripture. I am convinced, however, that the elusive search for *the* true, historical meaning of the text in actual fact places ordinary believers at the mercy of individual scholars, who rarely if ever come to exegetical agreement among one another. Moreover, the elusive search for the Bible's historical meaning downplays Scripture's intent to encounter the believer sacramentally as it is read.

By placing the word *Scripture* as the second element in each chapter title, I make the point that we properly uphold Scripture only if and when we acknowledge also the term that precedes it. I should, however, insert a caveat about the kind of claim I intend to make with the various titles. The type of claim is not identical in each case. The five pairings vary in kind and significance. While I'm convinced, for instance, that without the church there simply is no Scripture, I wouldn't dare make the claim that someone who rejects Christian Platonism cannot uphold Scripture's authority (though I do think authority looks far more attractive from a realist than from a nominalist standpoint). Still, in an important respect, each title does a similar thing. Each refers to something that has come under suspicion in the modern period—for example, a Christ-centered reading of Scripture, the centrality of the church for biblical exegesis, or heavenly contemplation as Scripture's ultimate aim. And in each case, I make it my goal to retrieve an important aspect of the Great Tradition's reading of Scripture, suggesting that our doctrine of Scripture suffers in some way when we fail to do justice to the first element of each chapter title.

Christ is the heart of all Scripture, and all Scripture points to him and makes him present. He is the reason we treat Scripture as authoritative and meaningful. So, in the first chapter I make the point that only by acknowledging Christ as Scripture's true content can we retain Scripture as Scripture. Hence the title of this chapter: "No Christ, No Scripture."

The same goes for the other four chapter titles. "No Plato, No Scripture" is meant to highlight that we all read Scripture through a metaphysical lens (whether we acknowledge it or not) and that Christian Platonism best allows us, by faith, to recognize Christ as the sacramental reality present in the biblical text. The sacramental hermeneutic of the Scriptures is dependent, or so I argue, on a Christian Platonist metaphysic.

The third chapter turns to the doctrine of providence ("No Providence, No Scripture"), and it points out that Scripture is treated rightly only when we do justice to its role in God's providential care. An acknowledgment of Scripture's place within divine providence recognizes that the Word of God shines through more clearly in Scripture than in any other human witness; Scripture participates in a unique manner in God's eternal Word, and it is this unique mode of participation that renders it special and authoritative for believers.

By linking Scripture to the church in the title of the fourth chapter ("No Church, No Scripture"), I aim to caution against academic elitism, arguing that the proper site for reading Scripture is not the university but the church. By allowing the academy to set the rules for biblical engagement, we have far too easily let methodological naturalism creep into our biblical interpretation. I make a plea, therefore, for a return to an ecclesial mode of reading Scripture, which allows canon, liturgy, and creed to shape how we understand the Bible. Again, my point is that the recognition of an ecclesial setting for biblical interpretation is a way of upholding rather than of undermining Scripture's unique and high position.

The title of the final chapter, "No Heaven, No Scripture," emphasizes that Scripture posits neither itself nor any other created good as our ultimate aim or telos. Scripture's sacramental truth is otherworldly, contemplative, heavenly. The modern turn away from contemplation toward a life of action flouts Scripture's true function and serves to undermine its sacramental role. Only when we read Scripture with a view to its ultimate, spiritual end—the beatific vision itself—do we do justice to its intended role. When we ignore or downplay Scripture's mediatory role in drawing us to the heavenly contemplation of God and reduce Scripture to a this-worldly guide in the service of political or social-justice concerns, we domesticate and naturalize it. Scripture is Scripture because of the heavenly future of God in Christ that it holds out to us.

The "five things" in this book's title may worry some readers that I have caved in to an instrumentalist or utilitarian approach to hermeneutics. Let me assure you: I have a strong dislike of "how-to" books, and in no way do I set out to provide yet another "method" on how to read the Bible. My aim is simply to offer a reminder of the theological focus of biblical exegesis. The unfortunate divide between biblical and doctrinal theology will disappear, I am convinced, wherever Christ is the theological starting point, center, and goal of our biblical engagement.

NO CHRIST, NO SCRIPTURE

SOLA SCRIPTURA AND CIRCULAR READING

Christ is first, Scripture second. From the beginning of the church's history, biblical interpreters have recognized that Scripture serves its regulative role for the church's faith because Christ is present on every page. This means that the early church's interpretation primarily moved from Christ to Scripture, not from Scripture to Christ. The purpose of this first chapter is to explain this claim as well as its implications. *The first thing that I, as a theologian, wish biblical scholars knew is that recognition of Christ's presence in Scripture is essential for upholding its authority.*

Discussions surrounding theological exegesis are often obstreperous because they continue to take place against the backdrop of Reformation debates about Scripture and tradition. Biblical scholars, especially evangelical biblical scholars, tend to be apprehensive about theological exegesis for fear that theological categories will override the sometimes-obvious meaning of the biblical text. Theological convictions that have developed over the course of history shape our reading of the text and, so it is thought, threaten to warp its original, true meaning. The perceived problem is that the Bible is forced to yield pride of place to tradition, so that human authority (tradition) ends up trumping divine authority (Scripture).

In this chapter, I purposely focus on the relationship not between Scripture and tradition but between Scripture and Christ.[1] This shift allows us to move the focus away from formal categories (the authority of Scripture vis-à-vis tradition) to material categories (the content of Scripture and tradition, which centers on Christ). I do not mean to suggest that the question of formal authority (the Scripture-tradition relationship) is insignificant or irrelevant to the discussion at hand. What I am suggesting, however, is that the question of formal authority is secondary, in the sense that what we say about Scripture and tradition depends on how we understand the question of Christ's presence in the Scriptures.[2]

In some quarters, the notion of *sola scriptura* has gained such prominence that agreement on formal authority becomes the main thing that unites us. As long as we share the basic conviction that Scripture alone governs our theological commitments, we are willing to tolerate many disagreements, because we are convinced that our shared belief in the authority of the Bible yields a "mere Christianity" that can accommodate varying convictions about secondary theological matters—including perhaps what we confess about the person of Christ, about the doctrine of the Trinity, or about the sacramental life of the church.[3]

---

[1]Both in this sentence and repeatedly in the rest of the chapter, I will use the term *Scripture* to refer to the entire Bible. At times, however, I will use *Scripture* to speak of the Old Testament (since this was the use of the term *Scripture* in the New Testament and the early fathers). Whenever I use the term in this more restrictive sense, the context will make this clear (often by explicitly referring to the Old Testament).

[2]See Yves Congar, *The Meaning of Tradition*, trans. A. N. Woodrow (1964; repr., San Francisco: Ignatius, 2004), 85-90.

[3]Even as thoughtful a writer as Kevin J. Vanhoozer turns the five *solas* of the Reformation into the "distinguishing marks of evangelicalism," which he also calls "mere Protestant Christianity." *Biblical Authority After Babel: Retrieving the Solas in the Spirit of Mere Protestant*

The church fathers—as well as theologians through most of the Great Tradition of the church—would have viewed such an approach to Scripture with a sense of bewilderment. Their focus was not on the formal authority but on the material contents of the Scriptures. Don't get me wrong: it is not the case that they disregarded the authority of Scripture or considered it unimportant. When reading Saint Irenaeus's arguments against the Gnostics, for example, one cannot but be impressed with the consistent appeal to Scripture. As is well known, one of his key objections to the Gnostics centers on their interpretation of biblical texts. Scripture is obviously central to Irenaeus's defense of orthodoxy.[4] Similarly, the fourth-century debates about the doctrine of the Trinity as well as the later Alexandrian-Antiochian arguments about the person of Christ centered on biblical exegesis. Scripture was central to the development of Christian doctrine.

Nonetheless, these patristic debates are marked by a kind of circularity. While Athanasius defended the divinity of the Son with biblical arguments, these arguments were linked closely to prior convictions that he held by faith. Athanasius was convinced that in approaching the Scriptures he knew its overall *dianoia*, that is, its "mind" or its meaning. Insight into the *dianoia* of Scripture allowed him to read it correctly—that is to say, it allowed him to discover how a particular passage fits within the overall *hypothesis* or "plot" of the Scriptures that the church's faith teaches. Francis Young gives an example of this in Athanasius's debate with the Arians.[5] In his *First Discourse Against the Arians*, the Egyptian bishop engages in a fairly lengthy discussion both of Psalm 45:7 ("You have loved righteousness

Christianity (Grand Rapids, MI: Brazos, 2016), *passim* (esp. 232). The problem here is that it is no longer Nicene Christianity but the five *solas* of the Reformation that are taken as the heart of the faith.

[4]For the centrality (and Christ-centeredness) of scriptural interpretation in Irenaeus, see John Behr, *The Way to Nicaea*, vol. 1 of *The Formation of Christian Theology* (Crestwood, NY: St. Vladimir's Seminary Press, 2001), 111-33.

[5]Frances M. Young, *Biblical Exegesis and the Formation of Christian Culture* (1997; repr., Peabody, MA: Hendrickson, 2002), 43-45.

and hated wickedness. *Therefore* God, your God, has anointed you with the oil of gladness beyond your companions") and of Philippians 2:8-9 ("He humbled himself by becoming obedient to the point of death, even death on a cross. *Therefore* God has highly exalted him and bestowed on him the name that is above every name"). Hebrews 1:8-9 explicitly identifies Christ as the bridegroom of Psalm 45, and the question—a potentially embarrassing one for pro-Nicene theologians such as Athanasius—was how this "anointing" of the Son would *not* imply his secondary status vis-à-vis the Father. The psalmist may give the impression that it is the Son's virtue that gave him his status of "anointed" one. Similarly, Saint Paul's Philippian hymn may seem to explain Christ's exaltation as Lord simply as the reward for his obedience (with both passages using the term *therefore*, giving virtue as the reason for the anointing or the exaltation).

Athanasius, however, applies the *dianoia* or "mind" of all of Scripture to Psalm 45:7 and Philippians 2:9, and it is worth examining in some detail how he does this.[6] The Alexandrian theologian asks rhetorically what the Savior was prior to the incarnation if it is true that he received the epithets of *God*, *Son*, and *Lord* only as a reward for his virtue. To show that these names cannot be restricted to Christ in his incarnation, Athanasius points to manifestations of the Son before the incarnation. If Christ was promoted merely as a reward for his virtue, asks Athanasius,

> how were all things made by Him [Col 1:16], or how in Him, were He not perfect, did the Father delight [Prov 8:30]? And He, on the other hand, if now promoted, how did He before rejoice in the presence of the Father [Prov 8:31]? And, if He received His worship after dying, how is Abraham seen to

---

[6]Peter J. Leithart observes that according to Athanasius, "Arian readings fail because they create dissonance in what should be a harmonious story—for instance, they deny that the Creator and Savior are one character." *Athanasius* (Grand Rapids, MI: Baker Academic, 2011), 40.

worship Him in the tent [Gen 18:2] and Moses in the bush
[Ex 3:6]? And, as Daniel saw, myriads of myriads, and thousands of thousands were ministering unto Him [Dan 7:10]?
And if, as they say, He had His promotion now, how did the Son
Himself make mention of . . . His glory before and above the
world, when He said, "Glorify Thou Me, O Father, with the
glory which I had with Thee before the world was" [Jn 17:5].[7]

Athanasius here appeals to the biblical truth that the Son preexisted
as the eternal Son of God during the old dispensation. The Son was
the Creator, the Wisdom of God who lived in the presence of God
and as such enjoyed the Father's glory. What is more, this eternal Son
of God manifested himself within the historical economy to saints
such as Abraham, Moses, and Daniel. This last point is significant,
and I will return to it momentarily. Athanasius interprets the Old
Testament theophanies christologically. They are proof of the glory
that the Son, in his preexistence, had with the Father.

Athanasius links this preexistence of the Son to soteriological convictions: only if the Savior had the status of God, Son, and Lord prior
to his incarnation does the theology of deification make sense. Athanasius questions how those who lived under the old dispensation could
be deified by Christ if Christ received his status as Son of God at the
end of his obedient life as a reward for it. Quoting John 10:35 ("If he
called them gods to whom the word of God came"), he continues:

If all that are called sons and gods, whether in earth or in heaven,
were adopted and deified through the Word, and the Son
Himself is the Word, it is plain that through Him are they all, and
He Himself before all, or rather He Himself only is very Son, and
He alone is very God from the very God, not receiving these
prerogatives as a reward for His virtue, nor being another beside
them, but being all these by nature and according to essence.[8]

---

[7]Athanasius, *Four Discourses Against the Arians* I.38 (NPNF 2/4:328).
[8]Athanasius, *Four Discourses Against the Arians* I.39 (NPNF 2/4:329).

For Athanasius, it is clear that in the *hypothesis* or plot of Scripture, the Son is preexistent and, therefore, does not receive the status of divinity as a reward for his virtue. Athanasius concludes from this that we must distinguish between Christ's divine and human natures. Passages such as Psalm 45:7 and Philippians 2:9 speak of his human nature: only human nature is such that it can be exalted, explains Athanasius: "The term in question, 'highly exalted,' does not signify that the essence of the Word was exalted, for He was ever and is 'equal to God,' but the exaltation is of the manhood."[9] Only Christ's human nature can be exalted, which in turn allows for the deification or exaltation of those who through faith are in Christ.

Athanasius refers to his interpretation as an "ecclesiastical sense" (*dianonan . . . ekklēsiastikēn*), which he contrasts with the "private sense" (*idion noun*) of his Arian opponents.[10] Athanasius's exegesis is guided by the sense (*dianoia*) that is in line with the church's confession of the two natures of Christ. Frances Young rightly refers in this connection to the canon of truth or the rule of faith as guiding the exegetical process.[11] "The 'Canon of Truth' or 'Rule of Faith' expresses the mind of Scripture," she comments, so for Athanasius "an exegesis that damages the coherence of that plot, that *hypothesis . . .* cannot be right."[12] Athanasius was convinced of the ecclesial understanding of the biblical plot, and even if some passages seemed a difficult fit within this plot he nonetheless was convinced he must interpret them in line with it.

A modern *sola scriptura* viewpoint may have a hard time justifying Athanasius's approach: the circularity that he assumes between Christ and Scripture may seem dangerously subjective. Doesn't Athanasius put his own, preconceived meaning onto the biblical text in order to uphold a pro-Nicene reading by hook or by crook? It is certainly true

---

[9]Athanasius, *Four Discourses Against the Arians* I.41 (*NPNF* 2/4:330).
[10]Athanasius, *Four Discourses Against the Arians* I.44 (*NPNF* 2/4:331); I.37 (*NPNF* 2/4:327).
[11]Young, *Biblical Exegesis*, 43.
[12]Young, *Biblical Exegesis*, 43.

that Athanasius refuses to isolate the scriptural passages at hand from the church's christological convictions, which is why he indeed engages in a circular type of argument. But I suspect that Athanasius didn't see this as a particularly troubling kind of circularity—and in light of the broad contemporary acknowledgment that all interpretation involves some kind of hermeneutical circle, Athanasius's approach should not cause undue surprise or offense.[13] The sense (*dianoia*) that he took from these passages was not just his own, subjective reader response. It was an *ecclesiastical* sense, which as such offered safeguards against the *private* interpretations of the Arians. A *sola scriptura* approach that rejects creedal guidelines as authoritative for interpretation for fear of circularity usually ends up with a far more serious case of circularity, for interpretation that claims to bracket theological preunderstanding (*Vorverständnis*) inevitably ends up smuggling in unacknowledged theological and metaphysical assumptions. When the individual biblical scholar neither acknowledges them nor is even aware of them, these subjective prior commitments tend to wreak exegetical and theological havoc. The church's confession is then erroneously viewed as lying at the end of a straight line rather than being caught up in a hermeneutical circle.

I already alluded to Athanasius's insistence that we should not only identify theological statements about the preexistence of the Son in the (Old Testament) Scriptures, but we should also interpret theophanies (divine appearances) and visions (to Abraham, Moses, and Daniel) christologically—that is, as Christophanies. In other words, on occasion the preexistent Son actually *manifested* himself to Old Testament saints. Both of these notions—the belief in the Son's preexistence and the christological exegesis of theophanies—seem to me highly significant in connection with our theme of "no Christ, no Scripture." Many biblical scholars, grounding themselves in a *sola*

---

[13]I have in mind especially the work of Hans-Georg Gadamer, *Truth and Method*, 2nd ed., trans. Joel Weinsheimer and Donald G. Marshal (1975; repr., London: Continuum, 2011).

scriptura doctrine, while ostensibly doing so in order to isolate Scripture and protect it against incursions of later tradition, actually isolate Scripture from Christ and shield it from a christological reading. On this view, after all, the main purpose of biblical interpretation is to reconstruct authorial intent; the meaning of the Scriptures lies in the past rather than the present. Christological and moral implications taken from the Old Testament are only later connections or applications. The meaning of the Old Testament Scriptures ceases to be inherently christological. As a result, one hears sermons from renowned Old Testament scholars that make little or no reference to Christ.

SENSUS PLENIOR AND REAL PRESENCE

To be sure, it is not as though Christology is entirely absent from such *sola scriptura* approaches to biblical interpretation. Christology comes to the fore in at least two ways. First, because many contemporary biblical scholars regard themselves as historians unearthing aspects of the redemptive-historical narrative, they do recognize Christ as the climax of that history.[14] The dramatic or narratival approaches to Scripture of scholars such as Craig Bartholomew and N. T. Wright treat the chronological unfolding of events (recorded in Scripture) in a purely historical manner—as a set of events that God may have orchestrated but that are not linked together at a higher, christological level. But this is a rather minimalist approach with significant shortcomings. Its fractured view of the biblical witness— one that metaphysically separates the Old Testament from the chronologically later Christ-event—cannot follow Saint Athanasius in his ecclesial recognition of the mind of Scripture. This contemporary *sola scriptura* hermeneutic fails to recognize the embeddedness of the ontological reality of the preexistent Christ within the Old

---

[14]One can think here, for instance, of N. T. Wright's *The Climax of the Covenant: Christ and the Law in Pauline Theology* (Minneapolis: Fortress, 1991). Wright often refers to his job as that of a historian.

Testament text. The nominalist preunderstanding undergirding this approach precludes a priori the real presence of Christ in the pages of the Old Testament Scripture.[15]

Second, such a *sola scriptura* hermeneutic will sometimes go beyond a strict separation between the Old Testament Scriptures and the Christ-event by acknowledging in addition to the authorial intent of a passage a fuller meaning, a *sensus plenior* that goes deeper than the original, historical meaning. As we will see, the notion of *sensus plenior* can be helpful as long as we apply it in a robust manner. The Catholic New Testament scholar Raymond Brown does precisely this when he takes the *sensus plenior* to mean "that additional, deeper meaning, intended by God but not clearly intended by the human author, which is seen to exist in the words of a biblical text (or group of texts, or even a whole book) when they are studied in the light of further revelation or development in the understanding of revelation."[16] On Brown's understanding, further revelation may clarify the deeper meaning of an earlier (Old Testament) text. John Goldingay gives a couple of examples of how such a *sensus plenior* functions within the Bible itself: God's prophecy to Ahaz in Isaiah 7:14 is explained by Matthew as referring to the virgin birth (Mt 1:23), and the Decalogue may be read as "containing in germ" Jesus' fuller revelation of God's will in the Sermon on the Mount (Mt 5–7).[17]

A *sola scriptura* hermeneutic, however, tends to be quite cautious with regard to the notion of *sensus plenior*. The fear is that it may give the interpreter's subjective insights a role in the interpretive process. Gordon Fee and Douglas Stuart insist that as a result of divine inspiration, New Testament authors were in a position to discern the

---

[15]Nominalism treats created objects (and historical events) as isolated particulars, while realism treats them as participating in universal forms or ideas—which in Christian metaphysics are usually understood christologically as cohering within the eternal Logos.

[16]Raymond E. Brown, *The Sensus Plenior of Sacred Scripture* (Baltimore, MD: St. Mary's University Press, 1955), 92.

[17]John Goldingay, *Approaches to Old Testament Interpretation* (1981; repr., Toronto: Clements, 1990), 108.

sensus plenior of the Old Testament Scriptures. Since we are not similarly inspired, however, we are not entitled to look for this deeper meaning in the way that the New Testament authors were. After discussing Paul's allegorical exegesis of 1 Corinthians 10:1-4, Fee and Stuart comment:

> We, however, are simply not inspired writers of Scripture. What Paul did we are not authorized to do. The allegorical connections he was inspired to find between the Old Testament and the New Testament are trustworthy. But nowhere does the Scripture say to us, "Go and do likewise." Thus the principle: *sensus plenior (fuller meaning) is a function of inspiration not illumination*.... Inspiration is the original motivation to record the Scripture in a certain way; illumination is the insight to understand what the Scripture's authors wrote. We cannot rewrite or redefine Scripture by our illumination. We can only perceive a *sensus plenior* with any certainty, therefore, *after the fact*. Unless something is identified as a *sensus plenior* in the New Testament, it cannot confidently be identified as such from the Old Testament by us on our own authority.[18]

Fee and Stuart do not seem entirely closed to discerning a *sensus plenior* that Scripture itself doesn't plainly disclose. It's just that we cannot arrive at it "confidently" or with "certainty." It is clear, however, that Fee and Stuart want to put the brakes on the perceived dangers of the allegorizing that tends to go hand in hand with the notion of *sensus plenior*.

The underlying question, I think, is this: When the New Testament detects a *sensus plenior* in the Old Testament, is this merely an instance of a New Testament *use* of the Old Testament, or does such a *sensus plenior* give us actual *exegetical* insights by entering into the

---

[18]Gordon D. Fee and Douglas Stuart, *How to Read the Bible for All Its Worth*, 4th ed. (Grand Rapids, MI: Zondervan, 2014), 209-10.

deeper (sacramental) *meaning* of the Old Testament?[19] I think it is the latter, but even if we were to restrict the term *exegesis* to a historical endeavor (trying to establish authorial intent), I do not see on what grounds such reconstructive activity should be our primary focus. Saint Paul appears interested in the *upbuilding* (*oikodomē*) of the church when he reads the (Old Testament) Scriptures. It is this same usefulness (*ōpheleia*; see 2 Tim 3:16) that determines the exegesis of theologians such as Saint Gregory of Nyssa.[20] In short, the New Testament authors and the subsequent tradition looked for the sacramental presence of Christ in the Old Testament. And they read the Scriptures in order to use them in the Christian life. This quest gives their exegesis a forward-looking movement in comparison to the backward-looking approach of much contemporary *sola scriptura* hermeneutics.

Christ, therefore, ought to be the starting point in our reading of the Scriptures—including the Old Testament. According to John's Gospel, it is only in the light of Christ's resurrection that the earlier Scriptures open up for us. When Jesus makes the "preposterous" claim that he will raise up the temple in three days (really talking about his body), the disciples don't understand; it is only after his resurrection that they remember he said this (Jn 2:22). When Jesus enters Jerusalem on a donkey in fulfillment of Zechariah's prophecy, the disciples don't get it; it is only "when Jesus was glorified" (Jn 12:16) that they "remembered" that these things had been written about him. In the same way, it is only once the Spirit of truth has come (Jn 15:26) that their persecution and martyrdom will make sense to them; then the disciples will remember (Jn 16:4) that Jesus told them about it. The disciples' memory—and their ability to understand the Scriptures—is linked

---

[19]Discourse about the New Testament's *use* of the Old Testament sometimes betrays a conviction that New Testament authors do not actually *interpret* the Old Testament.

[20]See Mark Sheridan, *Language for God in Patristic Tradition: Wrestling with Biblical Anthropomorphism* (Downers Grove, IL: IVP Academic, 2015), 226-29; Hans Boersma, *Embodiment and Virtue in Gregory of Nyssa* (Oxford: Oxford University Press, 2013), 68-69.

up with Jesus' resurrection, his glorification, and his giving of the Spirit of truth.[21]

It is possible for us as for the New Testament authors to search for and find the *sensus plenior*, the sacramental truth, of the Old Testament Scriptures because our knowledge of the risen Lord enables us to recognize how he is adumbrated in them. In faith we know our Lord as the original archetype, and therefore we can now discern his presence in the types that foreshadow him. The search for a *sensus plenior* is not an attempt to *impose* an alien meaning on the Old Testament Scriptures; it is rather a *discovery* of the real presence of the eternal Son of God who already makes his presence known, in anticipatory fashion, in the Old Testament Scriptures. Not to see Christ as already present there is to forgo their divinely intended purpose. "If you believed Moses," says Jesus to the Jews, "you would believe me; for he wrote of me" (Jn 5:46; see also Lk 24:27). Biblical scholarship suffers when it fails to recognize that Moses (and the rest of the Old Testament Scriptures) wrote primarily of Christ. And if it is true that we simply *discover* Christ as already present in the Scriptures, then it is appropriate to use sacramental language and say: Christ is the sacramental reality present within the Scriptures.

CHRISTOLOGICAL LITERALISM

I must express some reservations, therefore, with regard to Christopher Seitz's recent book, *The Elder Testament: Canon, Theology, Trinity*.[22] I do so with a degree of hesitancy since Seitz's canonical approach has much that is commendable. Seitz assures us we can legitimately search within the Old Testament Scriptures for the contents

[21]See William M. Wright and Francis Martin, *Encountering the Living God in Scripture: Theological and Philosophical Principles for Interpretation* (Grand Rapids, MI: Baker Academic, 2019), 222-25.
[22]Christopher R. Seitz, *The Elder Testament: Canon, Theology, Trinity* (Waco, TX: Baylor University Press, 2018). My discussion of Seitz's book here is mostly taken from Hans Boersma, "Christopher Seitz and the Priority of the Christ Event," *ProEccl* 29 (2020): 275-84.

of the Christian faith. He regards the Old Testament Scriptures themselves as the basis for our knowledge of Jesus Christ: "Jesus Christ the
Word is revealed as such by the prophets," Seitz boldly and rightly
claims.[23] This providential structuring of the Scriptures determines
Seitz's entire approach. His main emphasis is that the Old Testament
Scriptures themselves exert prospective theological "pressure." That is
to say, the Old Testament *demands* some rather than other interpretations. Time and again, this inherent pressure of the text yields for Seitz
a Christian theological reading of the Old Testament text. For example,
the monotheist confession of Isaiah 45:20-25 exerts pressure on the
acknowledgment in Philippians 2:5-11 that it is Jesus before whom
every knee shall bow.[24] Seitz argues, therefore, that the early church
neither invented the doctrine of the Trinity nor imposed its trinitarian
readings onto the Old Testament. On Seitz's reading, God himself
providentially inserts clues in the text that demand a trinitarian reading.

Seitz's repeated insistence that the Christian understanding of God
is embedded within the Old Testament's discourse about God strikes
me as profoundly true.[25] Reflecting on the Emmaus Road story in
Luke 24, Seitz rightly sees the risen Lord's interpretation of "all the
Scriptures" as implying that "the Lord was known here 'in figures and
under signs,'"[26] so that the Old Testament Scriptures manifest Christ
in their own way, distinct (though presumably not separate) from the
sacramental reality itself, seen only by the eyes of faith.[27] At this point,
Seitz appeals in a footnote to a beautiful quotation from the twentieth-
century Jesuit patristic scholar Henri de Lubac: "In the literal meaning
of Scripture, the Logos is not, properly speaking, incarnated as he
is in the humanity of Jesus, and this is what allows us still to speak
of a comparison: he is, nevertheless, already truly incorporated there;

[23]Seitz, *Elder Testament*, 27.
[24]Seitz, *Elder Testament*, 187.
[25]Seitz, *Elder Testament*, 12, 16.
[26]Seitz, *Elder Testament*, 180.
[27]Seitz, *Elder Testament*, 181.

he himself dwells there, not just some idea of him, and this is what authorizes us to speak already of his coming, of his *hidden presence*."[28] Seitz's language of *embedding* and of *sacramental reality* indicates that for him the New Testament reality is always already present in the Old Testament. Therefore, a Christian reading is not an arbitrary, ex post facto reading back into the Old Testament of what we already believed anyway. Seitz's sacramental approach seems to me right in important respects.

Still, he does insufficient justice to what de Lubac terms the *hidden* character of Christ's presence in the Old Testament. Concerned as he is to counter reader-response interpretations of the Old Testament, Seitz wants to insist that *when read literally* the Old Testament yields the ontological reality of the rule of faith. This results in a markedly strong emphasis on the discrete reality of the Old Testament itself. It receives a rather independent status vis-à-vis the New Testament reality, so much so that the Old Testament is for him primarily the Scriptures of *Israel*. Christians reading them are standing in the "hall of the Gentiles," as "invitees," "guests," "outsiders looking in," so that our stance as readers should be "one of caution, humility, and respect for our status as invitees."[29] Seitz reminds us that Jesus "opens the scriptures for his brethren and declares them to be everywhere about him, not about you and me."[30] By treating the Old Testament on its own, discrete terms, Seitz ends up treating the Old Testament only secondarily as the church's Scriptures: they are, for him, primarily the Scriptures of Israel.

Seitz believes that it is by means of a literal reading of the Old Testament that we arrive at the ontological reality (that is, the christological and trinitarian faith of the church) implied in the Old Testament. I am not convinced that the early church knew of such christological or trinitarian literalism. It knew of allegory (Christology),

---

[28]Seitz, *Elder Testament*, 181n2; emphasis added.
[29]Seitz, *Elder Testament*, 57, 60-61.
[30]Seitz, *Elder Testament*, 60.

tropology (morality), and anagogy (eschatology), and it saw these
various meanings as providentially hidden within the (Old Testament) Scriptures. On the early church's understanding, one could
arrive at these hidden, deeper levels only by a distinct illumination
of the Spirit. (As Seitz himself acknowledges in connection with Luke
24, it is only with eyes of faith that we recognize the sacramental
reality.)[31] The christological reality (*res*) of the Old Testament sacrament (*sacramentum*) was hidden, and it is not the case that just
anyone is able to recognize it.

The pervasive acknowledgment among the church fathers of the
need for spiritual discernment makes clear their belief that the reader
gains the ability to discover Christ in the Old Testament text only
when the reader is transfigured by the reality of Christ. Origen goes
so far as to identify eating the Passover lamb (Ex 15) with the allegorical reading of Scripture, so that with Christ we "pass over" into
the heavenly realm as we read the Scriptures allegorically or spiritually,
rather than merely literally or physically. Whatever we may think of
Origen's exegesis of Exodus 15, it is clear that he was convinced one
needs spiritual insight to discover Christ in the Scriptures. We have
already seen that for Athanasius only an ecclesiastical mind (*dianoia*)
offers genuine insight into the Scriptures. And Gregory of Nyssa's
invective against Eunomius as a "slave of the letter" who "attends in
Jewish fashion to the mere sound of syllables" and is a mere "scribbler"
has to do with Eunomius's (neo-)Arian conviction that one must read
Proverbs 8 literally rather than allegorically. The Eunomians do not
do justice to the hidden (*kekrymmenōs*) or allegorical manner in
which proverbs communicate.[32] For the early church, someone
without Christ remains in an important sense without the Scriptures,
since Christ is their key. The christological allegorizing of the Fathers

---

[31]Seitz, *Elder Testament*, 181.
[32]See further Hans Boersma, *Scripture as Real Presence: Sacramental Exegesis in the Early
Church* (Grand Rapids, MI: Baker Academic, 2017), 97-102, 159-86.

(which we may also call "sacramental exegesis") was their stock-in-trade, and its basic rule was simple: no Christ, no Scripture.

Seitz is right: a purely historical (or dramatic) approach to Scripture is deeply problematic, and given its influence in biblical scholarship, we need Seitz's polemic. Still, the ontological reality of which Seitz speaks (i.e., Christ) assumes flesh in the new covenant within history. That is to say, the ontological reality is revealed in time, in the incarnation, as the climax of the covenant (to use Wright's term). And because the ontological reality has taken on flesh in time, we cannot ignore the salvation-historical thrust of Scripture. Biblical scholars do not go wrong by drawing attention to Scripture's horizontal, salvation-historical thrust; they merely go wrong when they assume it precludes the vertical, sacramental presence of the mystery of Christ in prior sacramental figures. For de Lubac (as well as the Fathers and medieval theologians whose mouthpiece he was), it is in and through the historical *factum Christi* as the focal point of salvation history that we get to know the ontological reality of the faith.

Furthermore, it is only *because the believer already knows the ontological reality* of the faith that he is now able to discern Christ's presence also within the Old Testament as its deepest allegorical truth. Only faith in Christ allows us to look back and recognize the pressure that emanates from the Old Testament witness with regard to the reality of Christ. Seitz is right to draw our attention to the theological pressure of the Old Testament text. But this pressure is not necessarily visible from the surface of the text. Christ's presence in the Old Testament is not equally accessible for Christians and non-Christians. The pressure Seitz mentions is something we recognize only through the eyes of faith.

For de Lubac, discerning the reality of the Christ-event in the pages of the Old Testament Scripture was not a matter of christological literalism; it was, rather, a matter of christological allegorizing. The Old Testament truth is hidden and needs to be uncovered by means of allegory. Theologians such as Athanasius, Basil of Caesarea, and Gregory of Nyssa did not engage in exegetical debates about specific Old Testament passages because they were convinced that at a purely natural level they might arrive at agreement with their opponents. Rather, they did so because (1) they wanted to shore up the faith of the church internally against heretical attacks from those who could no longer see the truth of the gospel, a protective measure addressed to those already possessing spiritual eyes to see; and (2) they hoped, presumably, that the Spirit might through the debate give heretics an understanding of the truth of the gospel, a proactive measure addressed to those not yet possessing spiritual eyes to see. As a result, the heretics, too, might recognize the reality of the faith in passages such as Proverbs 8. The internal pressure of the Old Testament text cannot be discerned equally by all—it is faith that sensitizes one to the christological reality that the church claims to be present in the Old Testament witness.

TYPOLOGY AND ALLEGORY

Scholars sometimes distinguish between typology and allegory. Here the assumption is that in typological exegesis one looks for similarities between chronologically distinct events (both conveyed in Scripture), while allegorizing arbitrarily and without warrant imposes an alien meaning onto the text. Now, *sola scriptura* biblical scholars are not necessarily opposed to typology. N. T. Wright, for instance, bases his theological insights in good part on typology, despite disavowing the notion.[33] His now-famous thesis that Second Temple Jews thought

---

[33]Wright comments that Paul's rereading of monotheism, election, and eschatology is not "a matter merely of typology, picking a few earlier themes and watching the same patterns repeat themselves, though this also happens often enough. . . . Paul had in mind an essentially historical and sequential reading of scripture, in which the death and resurrection of the Messiah formed the unexpected but always intended climax of God's lengthy plan." *Paul: In Fresh Perspective* (Minneapolis: Fortress, 2009), 84-85. In actual fact, Wright's reading of Paul's theology is markedly typological (a notion that presupposes historical sequence). Wright often speaks of Christ's "reconstitution" of Israel, which functions remarkably similar to Irenaeus's "recapitulation," which I discuss below. Both notions are typological in structure.

of themselves as still being in exile operates within a broader typological frame. For Wright, the true return from exile takes place in Christ's death and resurrection, so that the Babylonian exile corresponds to his death and resurrection as type to antitype. Christ, in that sense, may be said to have suffered on our behalf the exilic curse on the cross.

Wright does something similar with the exodus, treating the historical exodus from Egypt as a type of the exodus that Christ has performed through his resurrection—the related antitype.[34] To be sure, typology does not function in quite the same way with regard to the exodus as it does in terms of exile. For Wright, the exodus from Egypt and the exodus from sin and death are historically separate, with the former serving as a type of the latter. The return from Babylonian exile, on the other hand, is indistinguishable from Christ's resurrection: because Wright sees the former as continuing at the time of Christ, he treats the two as one and the same. Because he believes that for the Jews the exile had never truly come to an end, Wright can speak of Christ's death as Israel's exile and of his resurrection as Israel's return from exile. So, Wright's exodus typology treats type and antitype as historically separate, while his exile typology regards them as identical.

As we will see, it is of some importance how we treat the type-antitype relationship. For now, let me simply observe that typological exegesis is not uncommon among biblical scholars.[35] To my mind,

---

[34]I discuss Wright's approach to the exodus in "Sacramental Interpretation: On the Need for Theological Grounding of Narratival History," in *Exile: A Conversation with N. T. Wright*, ed. James M. Scott (Downers Grove, IL: IVP Academic, 2017), 255-72.

[35]See, for instance, R. T. France, *Jesus and the Old Testament: His Application of Old Testament Passages to Himself and His Mission* (1971; repr., Vancouver, BC: Regent College Publishing, 1998), 38-80; Walter C. Kaiser, *The Uses of the Old Testament in the New* (1985; repr., Eugene, OR: Wipf & Stock, 2001), 101-10; Douglas J. Moo, "The Problem of *Sensus Plenior*," in *Hermeneutics, Authority, and Canon*, 2nd ed., D. A. Carson and John D. Woodbridge (Grand Rapids, MI: Baker, 1995), 195-98; David L. Baker, *Two Testaments, One Bible: The Theological Relationship Between the Old and New Testaments*, 3rd ed. (Downers Grove, IL: InterVarsity Press, 2010), 169-90.

this is as it should be. Scripture itself leads the way in typological interpretation, treating historically later events as similar to earlier ones despite the historical distance separating them. These kinds of patterns of similarity occur repeatedly, even within the Old Testament itself, particularly among the prophets, who often compare the promised future to earlier events in the history of Israel. When they do so, the anticipated future invariably outdoing the original historical event in glory—put in terms of analogy, the dissimilarity is greater than the similarity.[36] The Gospels and Pauline letters also engage in a kind of typological interpretation of the Christ-event. Most famously, perhaps, Matthew's Gospel repeatedly treats the events in the life of Christ as typologically connected to the history of Israel.[37] But Saint Paul, too, interprets the Christ-event against the backdrop both of Adam's and of Israel's history. Christ is the second Adam, after all (Rom 5:12; 1 Cor 15:21-22); and much of Paul's soteriological terminology—terms such as *calling, election, redemption, adoption,* etc.—takes its meaning from Israel's Old Testament story of salvation. The typological relationship is so pervasive that like fish in the water we often don't even notice the figural environment within which our theology makes sense. I could go on to talk about typology in the letter to the Hebrews and in Revelation, but I think the point has been sufficiently made. Typology makes sense both of relationships within the Old Testament itself and of the relationship between Old and New Testaments.

The two uses of typology are, in fact, one and the same. The reason that the prophets employ typology is largely that they use historical events to point to the climactic unfolding of history in the messianic future. So, when the New Testament treats the Christ-event as the

---

[36]Jean Daniélou often uses the language of similarity and dissimilarity to illuminate the relationship between type and antitype (or archetype). See Hans Boersma, *Nouvelle Théologie and Sacramental Ontology: A Return to Mystery* (Oxford: Oxford University Press, 2009), 178-80.

[37]See Peter J. Leithart, *Jesus as Israel*, vol. 1 of *The Gospel of Matthew Through New Eyes* (Monroe, LA: Athanasius Press, 2017).

eschatological climax that, at the same time, is the great antitype to earlier types, it has in mind the very same antitype that the prophets envisaged. Indeed, when the New Testament identifies the Christ-event as inaugurating the kingdom of God, it makes clear that the prophetic promises of the great antitype have now come to fruition and that the eschaton of the messianic future has arrived.

Such a reading of typology undergirds the Christian theological project from its inception. Saint Irenaeus, in his late second-century anti-Gnostic writings, employed a form of typology commonly referred to as recapitulation, a concept central both to his understanding of soteriology and to his interpretation of Scripture. For Irenaeus, Christ was typologically related to Adam—and hence to all humanity—so that in his faithful retracing of Adamic existence Christ, as our head (*caput*), saved all who are included in his person and work.[38] Inasmuch as Christ resisted temptation where Adam had failed the test, Christ was able to undo the fall and to perfect or mature humanity in his own person. But Christ not only recapitulated all of humanity; he also recapitulated the (Old Testament) Scriptures. Irenaeus objected to Gnostic and Marcionite exegesis precisely because it failed to recognize that the Scriptures have been recapitulated in Christ as their climactic aim or purpose. For the bishop of Lyons, the Law and the Prophets find their point of unity in Christ. And so, Irenaeus insists that Christ "was sold with Joseph, and He guided Abraham; was bound along with Isaac, and wandered with Jacob; with Moses He was a Leader, and, respecting the people, Legislator. He preached in the prophets."[39] Joseph, Abraham, Isaac, Jacob, and Moses were all types recapitulated in and by Christ.

---

[38]Irenaeus borrows the term recapitulation from Eph 1:10, which speaks of God's plan "to unite (*anakephalaiōsasthai*) all things in [Christ], things in heaven and things on earth." The term *recapitulation* is a literal translation of the Greek *anakephalaiōsis*, both terms containing the word *head* (*caput* or *kephalē*).

[39]Irenaeus, *Fragments from the Lost Writings of Irenaeus* 54 (ANF 1:577).

Both soteriologically and hermeneutically, recapitulation bridges the distance between type and antitype. For Irenaeus, as earlier for Melito of Sardis and Justin Martyr, recapitulation implies real presence: Christ was sold with Joseph, guided Abraham, was bound with Isaac, etc. Christ was really present in the earlier types. For Irenaeus, therefore, to interpret the Old Testament Scriptures is to search in them for the hidden presence of Christ:

> If anyone, therefore, reads the Scriptures with attention, he will find in them an account of Christ, and a foreshadowing of the new calling (*vocationis*). For Christ is the treasure that was hid (*thesaurus absconsus*) in the field [Mt 13:44], that is, in this world (for "the field is the world"); but the treasure hid in the Scriptures is Christ, since He was pointed out by means of types and parables. ... When it [i.e., the law] is read by the Christians, it is a treasure, hid indeed in a field, but brought to light by the cross of Christ.[40]

For Irenaeus, Christ is the treasure hidden in the Scriptures, and our task as readers is to find him there. In other words, the relationship between type and fulfillment is not just historical; it is primarily sacramental. Christ was really present both within history and within the Scriptures. For Irenaeus, we could say, Christ is the treasure hidden within the depths of Scripture. The maxim "no Christ, no Scripture" is Irenaean in its provenance.

At its most basic level, therefore, typology does not move from earlier type to later antitype (though, to be sure, there is such a historical unfolding), but from original archetype (Christ-event) to types (shadowy reflections). Though historical types may *chronologically* foreshadow Christ, *ontologically* they follow him and are patterned on him. No matter where we are in salvation history, Christ is always the *archē*, the origin and principle, since in the incarnation

---

[40]Irenaeus, *Against Heresies* 4.26.1 (*ANF* 1:496). The Latin within the first set of round brackets is in the original text; square brackets are added.

God has made himself present in Christ by way of hypostatic union. What God does historically in and through the Christ-event, therefore, constitutes the archetype on which all of history is patterned and in which it is grounded. The biblical typologies that I mentioned earlier are not just interesting similarities. They are providentially ordered. Since God's eternal plan is manifest most clearly in Christ (see Heb 1:1)—or, put differently, since Christ is the Alpha and the Omega— the historical unfolding of Adamic and Israelite history is but the shadow of the reality that is God in Christ. I won't object to the language of *antitype*, therefore, but we need to recognize Christ as *archetype* if we are to understand how it is that typology functions metaphysically and hermeneutically.

It should be clear now where the twentieth-century distinction between typology and allegory went wrong. It is simply not the case that the Bible is typological, historical, horizontal, and hence reliable, while patristic and medieval interpretation is largely allegorical, abstract, vertical, and as such arbitrary. For the early church, typology functions *because* it speaks *other* (*allēgoreuein*, meaning "to speak other"). The basic Christian confession that Jesus is Lord (*kyrios*, the Septuagint term for Yahweh) is an allegorical claim that grounds all subsequent allegorical exegesis. This claim reads the Old Testament in a way it had never been read before. For the early church, allegorical exegesis was warranted, even demanded, by the incarnation. This claim does not warrant each and every allegorical interpretation, regardless of the detailed manner in which it is performed and no matter what the reader may think lies "hidden" in the text. It is rather to say that Christian allegorizing, despite its formal similarity to (and even its borrowing from) Philonic exegesis, takes its starting point not in Greek philosophy but in God's self-revelation in Christ.[41] As the archetype, he is the historic revelation

---

[41]Henri de Lubac points out that despite the similarities between the exegesis of the first-century Jewish Middle Platonist Philo and that of early Christian theologians such as

of God's providential plan, in which salvation history is anchored. For the church fathers, typology and allegory were identical because they refused to acknowledge history as a purely *this*-worldly unfolding of historical events, recognizing instead history's grounding in something *other*-worldly, a discovery that required *other* speech—allegory.

We see an interesting example of the centrality of Christ to biblical exegesis in the twelfth-century theologian William of Saint Thierry. In his article on this twelfth-century Benedictine monk, Andrew Louth explains why spiritual senses are required to recognize the mystery of the Scriptures.[42] William treats Christ as *Ursakrament*, describing him as "the best medicine to heal the tumor of our pride, the profound sacrament for our redemption and the forgiveness of sins."[43] To William, if Christ is a sacrament (*the* sacrament), this means that when he gives himself to us in the sacraments, he strengthens our spiritual, inmost being so that we can discern the divine truth of Christ:

> God is more intimate to us than our inmost being; for our outer being, that is, the senses of the body, he establishes for us the external sacraments through which he would lead our inmost being to his inmost being. Through the workings of the physical sacraments he gradually excites in us spiritual grace. It is for this purpose that he humbled himself to fellowship with our humanity: that he might make us partakers of his divinity.[44]

Origen, the latter looked for Christ as the deeper meaning of the text. For early Christians, therefore, allegorizing was not a neutral "method" but was grounded in Christology. See de Lubac, *Medieval Exegesis: The Four Senses of Scripture*, trans. Marc Sebanc and E. M. Macierowski (Grand Rapids, MI: Eerdmans, 1998, 2000), 1:149-50; 2:100-107; "Hellenistic Allegory and Christian Allegory," in *Theological Fragments*, trans. Rebecca Howell Balinski (San Francisco: Ignatius, 1989), 165-73.

[42]Andrew Louth, "William of St Thierry and Cistercian Spirituality," *DR* 102 (1984): 268-69. The following paragraphs are closely patterned on Louth's article.

[43]William of Saint Thierry, *The Mirror of Faith*, trans. Thomas X. Davis, Cistercian Fathers 15 (Kalamazoo, MI: Cistercian Publications, 1979), par. 23 (56).

[44]William of Saint Thierry, *Mirror of Faith*, par. 20 (49).

It is the sacraments that give us a taste of God's love, and it is the sacrament of the incarnation that allows us to recognize in Christ the very wisdom (*sapientia*) of God: "By increasing faith and illuminating grace, the knowledge of these temporal things is transformed into the wisdom of things eternal and the realities of time are clothed with the grace of eternity, when Christ Jesus begins not only to be perceived according to the flesh but to be understood according to his deeds and esteemed according to his works."[45] For William, therefore, it requires spiritual taste (*sapor*) to discern the sacramental reality of divine wisdom (*sapientia*) in Christ. William comments: "The mind is a particular strength of the soul whereby we cleave to God and enjoy God. This enjoyment, however, is a sort of divine savor, so wisdom (*sapientia*) comes from savor (*sapor*)."[46] For William, the Old Testament surface gives us only the outward *sacramentum*. We see this in the fact that the Old Testament gives only four of the five senses: "The eyes are the angels because of the loftiness of contemplation. The ears are the patriarchs because of the virtue of obedience [*obedire* being derived from *audire*, "to hear"]. The nose or smell is the prophets because of their awareness of absent realities. Touch is a sense common to all."[47] The insufficiency of Old Testament history is mirrored in the absence of the notion of taste from the Old Testament.

Taste is not absent from William's program, however: it is located in the incarnation. He immediately adds that taste is needed to support the body as a whole, so that without taste, the body remains dead. He comments that "a certain sweetness of savor follows upon taste, which the soul feels within her inner self in a singular way that is incommunicable to the other senses."[48] Taste is not simply a fifth sense. It is the sense that sacramentally mediates understanding of

---

[45]William of Saint Thierry, *Mirror of Faith*, par. 25 (59-60).
[46]William of Saint Thierry, *The Nature and Dignity of Love*, trans. Thomas X. Davis (Kalamazoo, MI: Cistercian Publications, 1981), par. 28 (88).
[47]William of Saint Thierry, *Nature and Dignity of Love*, par. 29 (88-89).
[48]William of Saint Thierry, *Nature and Dignity of Love*, par. 29 (89).

the Old Testament. William associates taste with the throat, which is located between the head and the body, and he suggests that Christ is similarly the means of grace that mediates between the body (law) and the head (grace): "Coming after the prophets and patriarchs as the boundary line between the law and grace, between the head and the body, he brought out through the mystery of his humanity and passion and resurrection whatever in the law and the prophets and the psalms was vital and useful to the body."[49] William of Saint Thierry considers Christ to be the archetype that gives access to the inner meaning of the Old Testament types:

> This is the taste which the Spirit of understanding gives us in Christ, namely, the understanding of Scripture and of the sacraments of God. . . . For when we begin not only to understand but even somehow, I say, to touch and handle the inner meaning of Scriptures and the virtue of God's mysteries and sacraments with the hand of experience . . . then at last wisdom accomplishes what is proper to it.[50]

Our sense of taste (which for William is code for the spiritual senses) is congruous with Christ's eternal wisdom. We discern the sacramental reality of the Scriptures when the taste of Christ's wisdom brings out the inner flavor of the Old Testament Scriptures.

CONCLUSION

Perhaps the most troubling shortcoming of a *sola scriptura* hermeneutic is that it fails to treat exegesis as a spiritual discipline. This is not to say that grammatical-historical exegetes have no place for prayer or for reliance on the Spirit in exegesis. I have no doubt that as Bible-believing Christians, these biblical scholars rely on divine guidance in their work. The problem, however, is that this is not seen

---

[49]William of Saint Thierry, *Nature and Dignity of Love*, par. 30 (90).
[50]William of Saint Thierry, *Nature and Dignity of Love*, par. 31 (91).

as making a difference to the exegetical outcome; there is no inherent link between spiritual wisdom and exegesis. By contrast, if the purpose of exegesis is to discern Christ—in the full, spiritual sense of tasting his wisdom—then it is impossible to regard the process as a detached historical method that arrives at its aim with the determination of authorial intent.

A *sola scriptura* hermeneutic typically excoriates illegitimate attempts to use later tradition as a lens for reading Scripture. As a remedy against undue reverence for tradition, biblical scholars typically appeal to *sola scriptura*. Certainly, the debates over Scripture and tradition are real, and they are significant. But perhaps the most serious victim of a radical *sola scriptura* approach is not the role of tradition but a christological reading of the text. When biblical scholars employ a *sola scriptura* hermeneutic, they often do so in order to safeguard authorial intent as the aim of interpretation. Exegesis thus changes from a theological to a historical discipline. For our interpretation of the Old Testament, this means that from the outset we preclude the possibility of the presence of Christ. The troubling result of such a *sola scriptura* view is the loss of Christ as Scripture's deepest truth and reality.

For Christians, the Bible is Holy Scripture because it is a sacrament that renders Christ present. To be sure, the multiple books that make up our Bible can be read for a variety of purposes. These purposes are not always out of place: it is possible and legitimate to read these books to learn about ancient Near Eastern history, to discover sources behind the text, or to investigate early Christian ecclesial practices. But the books of the Bible obtain their status as Holy Scripture only in relation to Christ. When we bracket or perhaps exclude Christ as the deepest reality of the biblical books, we fail to recognize the sacramental reality that unites them, and we lose their status as Scripture. No Christ, no Scripture.

NO PLATO, NO SCRIPTURE

METAPHYSICS AND SCRIPTURE

Without metaphysics—specifically, without a good dose of Plato—it becomes difficult to retain the teaching of Scripture. Christians should not treat Plato as a sheer villain, because a proper reading of Scripture depends in part on the traditional mode of reading it, which we may fairly label "Christian Platonist." My claim here is not exactly parallel to that of the previous chapter: I argued there that in biblical interpretation we move primarily from Christ to Scripture rather than from Scripture to Christ, so that without prior faith in Christ Scripture loses its regulative grounding. The maxim "No Plato, No Scripture" does not function in this same manner. As we will see, Plato does not have the same kind of priority that Christ has. On my understanding, a Christian metaphysic is theological in character: we dare not impose the pagan philosophy of Plato (or of anyone else) on Holy Scripture. Christian metaphysics must take its starting point in the Christian confession of Christ as the incarnate Lord. Still, it is true that the early church typically read Scripture through the metaphysical lens of

Christian Platonism, and I will argue that this approach safeguards rather than hampers biblical teaching. *The second thing that I, as a theologian, wish biblical scholars knew is that the Bible cannot be interpreted without prior metaphysical commitments and that we need Christian Platonism as an interpretive lens in order to uphold Scripture's teaching.*

It may be helpful at the outset to mention two questions I encounter most often when the topic of Christian Platonism comes up. The first is this: Doesn't Christian Platonism introduce a metaphysic that is alien to Scripture and as such obscures and perhaps even undermines its teaching? The second question comes up with people who are more or less satisfied that perhaps Christian Platonism isn't as troubling as initially thought. They nonetheless often raise a follow-up question: Do we need Platonism as a metaphysic today? Doesn't each historical era have its own metaphysical insights, and isn't it one of Christianity's distinct characteristics that it adapts to a variety of philosophical and metaphysical frameworks, so that our contemporary historical and cultural context demands a different, non-Platonic metaphysical lens for reading Scripture?

It would be a mistake simply to gloss over the first question. We must take it seriously because the danger of imposing an alien metaphysic on Scripture is by no means imaginary. We could potentially be taken in by all sorts of philosophical and metaphysical notions (see Col 2:8) and be tempted to read Scripture through their lens. This danger is no less real today than it was in the past. We are increasingly inclined to think that our particular situatedness determines our outlook on life and, therefore, our interpretation of Scripture. The underlying postmodern assumption is that we lack a shared rationality with which to approach the text. We have become convinced that we are primarily shaped by our economic, racial, and sexual identities and that these realities define all of our thinking and acting. But taking such identity markers as the key factor in interpretation inevitably yields a cacophony of voices. The resulting quest for individual (or group) validation of our subjective perspective leads to disagreements and clashes. Shared understanding becomes difficult, and mutual goodwill is taxed to the limit, with competing claims vying for recognition. All of which is to say that we should be alert to the pitfall of submitting Scripture to a metaphysic that is foreign to its basic teaching. It should also be clear, therefore, that if I am convinced that Christian Platonism is no such submission, I will have to make a positive case for it.

It is important not to skip over the truth element in the postmodern approach that I sketched in the previous paragraph. This approach rightly rejects a Cartesian separation between the human subject as "thinking substance" (*res cogitans*) and its surroundings as physical substance (*res extensa*).[1] The soul is not a separated self—or, in Charles Taylor's terms, a buffered self—with objective, rational access to the material world.[2] The radical dualism of Descartes's approach erroneously tries to shield the mind from its surroundings as if it were able objectively and neutrally to interpret a world of pure nature (*pura natura*).[3] We always interpret from a given situation, and we can never avoid a hermeneutical or interpretive stance. It is true, for instance, that a black woman in nineteenth-century America would have appropriated the Israelites' deliverance in the exodus differently than I do today as a white seminary professor.

The problem with the postmodern approach sketched above is not that it admits that we are interpretive creatures; the problem is

---

[1] See René Descartes, "Second Meditation," in *Discourse on Method and the Meditations*, trans. and ed. F. E. Sutcliffe (Hammondsworth, UK: Penguin, 1968), 102-12.
[2] See Charles Taylor, *A Secular Age* (Cambridge, MA: Belknap, 2007), 37-42, 134-42, 300-307.
[3] The notion of "pure nature" (*pura natura*) was first introduced into theology by the Catholic theologian Robert Bellarmine in the seventeenth century. It denotes an understanding of nature as strictly separate from supernatural grace. By viewing nature as strictly separate from supernatural grace, it becomes autonomous and has its own, this-worldly ends, separate from the supernatural end of the beatific vision. The notion of *pura natura*, therefore, was a major plank in the rise of secular modernity. See Hans Boersma, *Nouvelle Théologie and Sacramental Ontology: A Return to Mystery* (Oxford: Oxford University Press, 2009), 90-93.

that it errs in its determination of which identity is primary in interpretation. For Christians it is not income, color, age, or sex that determines our identity at its most basic level; our being in Christ (*en Christō*) takes priority over each of these factors. This is why Saint Paul insists that once we have put on Christ, "there is neither Jew nor Greek, there is neither slave nor free, there is no male and female," since we are all "one in Christ Jesus" (Gal 3:28). This doesn't mean that in Christ we lose our social, cultural, or sexual identity, but it does mean that these features are no longer primary and therefore should no longer determine our hermeneutical stance in life.

My appeal to Pauline theology implies that a Christian metaphysic must be theologically shaped. It will not do simply to import Plato (or later Platonism) and to read Scripture through such a Platonic lens. That would be an offense against the Pauline notion that our inclusion in Christ precedes everything else, including our interpretation of Scripture (as we have seen in chapter one). I will need to say more, therefore, about the way in which Christianity and Platonism relate to each other if I want to avoid falling into the trap of foisting a nontheological, nonchristological metaphysic on our reading of Scripture.[4] At the same time, however, the acknowledgment of a hermeneutical (Christ-grounded) interpretive starting point implies a particular metaphysical stance and as such underlines that there is no such thing as a reading of Scripture without metaphysics. Whether it is postmodern, neo-Marxist identity politics, modern rationalism in the Cartesian tradition, or Christian Platonism, each of these approaches has its own, distinct metaphysical stance. We all do metaphysics—it's just that some of us don't recognize this, confusing a *sola scriptura* approach with a non-metaphysical hermeneutic.

---

[4]For an excellent defense of the compatibility of Christian Platonism with the Old Testament, see Robin A. Parry, *The Biblical Cosmos: A Pilgrim's Guide to the Weird and Wonderful World of the Bible* (Eugene, OR: Cascade, 2014).

CHRISTIAN PLATONISM AND ANTINOMINALISM

What exactly do I mean by "Christian Platonism"? Lloyd Gerson's discussion of "Ur-Platonism" (literally, "proto-Platonism") may be helpful here.[5] Gerson uses the term to refer to an underlying shared set of five characteristics that all forms of Platonism have in common—indeed, the five characteristics were basic metaphysical building blocks for early Christian doctrine that have continued to serve as important ingredients in Christian Platonism ever since: (1) antimaterialism claims that bodies and their properties are not the only things that exist; (2) antimechanism maintains that the natural order (including, therefore, physical events) cannot be fully explained by physical or mechanical causes; (3) antinominalism argues that reality is made up not just of individuals, each uniquely situated in time and space, but that two individual objects can be the same in essence (e.g., both being canine) while still being unique individuals (distinct dogs); (4) antirelativism rejects the notion, both in terms of knowledge and morals, that human beings are the measure of all things, suggesting instead that goodness is a property of being; and (5) antiskepticism maintains that the real can in some manner become present to us, so that knowledge is within reach.[6]

Each of these five metaphysical claims has historically been vital to the Christian tradition. They are not Christian doctrines in and of themselves. But they are theoretical building blocks without which Christian doctrines are difficult or impossible to uphold. To reduce the Christian faith to a strictly biblical Christianity (let's call it *pura scriptura*) shorn of the metaphysical assumptions of Ur-Platonism is self-defeating.[7] While biblical scholars often undertake

---

[5]Lloyd P. Gerson, *From Plato to Platonism* (Ithaca, NY: Cornell University Press, 2013), 9-19. See also the discussion of Gerson's "Ur-Platonism" in Craig A. Carter, *Interpreting Scripture with the Great Tradition: Recovering the Genius of Premodern Exegesis* (Grand Rapids, MI: Baker Academic, 2018), 79-81.

[6]Gerson outlines the five characteristics in *From Plato to Platonism*, 11-14.

[7]I use the notion of *pura scriptura* to denote an approach that isolates Scripture from elements that have traditionally been regarded as illuminating biblical meaning—most notably metaphysics, tradition, and ecclesial context.

such antimetaphysical approaches to the Christian faith out of a genuine concern to uphold biblical authority, the effect is, in reality, its opposite: scriptural truth cannot be maintained without the five elements of Ur-Platonism.

A simple thought experiment makes clear why this is so. Try to assume, for a moment, a materialist or a relativist position. How can the claim that only bodies and their properties exist coincide with the biblical confession that God is Spirit (Jn 4:24), or that our bodies will take on immortality and incorruptibility (1 Cor 15:53-54)? Or how can the suggestion that human beings are the measure of all things jibe with the biblical notion of divine sovereignty and with the notion that we are meant to live out God's call on our lives—by way of divine laws and the gift of the Spirit? It should be clear that when all five elements of Ur-Platonism are rejected, we end up with a secular world of *pura natura* in which this-worldly objects and events are explained strictly on their own, this-worldly terms.

Each of the five characteristics is a significant building block of Ur-Platonism in its own right, and it would be a good exercise to trace their compatibility with biblical teaching.[8] But the antinominalist element is one that needs particular attention since it is antinominalism (or, put positively, realism) that undergirds each of the other elements of Ur-Platonism and that perhaps most obviously enters into Christian doctrinal formulations. Realism assumes that universals are real and that the objects of sense perception (human beings included) have being by participating in universals—what Plato termed "Forms" or "Ideas." In Christian theology, these Forms or Ideas are typically explained in a christological manner: the Son as the Word of the Father eternally contains all species within himself. The result is that two objects share the same essence (two people both belonging to the

---

[8]Paul Tyson helpfully points out the similarities between Platonic metaphysics and Pauline theology in *Returning to Reality: Christian Platonism for Our Times*, Kalos Series 2 (Eugene, OR: Cascade, 2014), 78-89.

species of humanity, or two dogs both belonging to the canine species) without being identical.[9] Through a variety of developments in the late Middle Ages, this realist perspective gradually gave way to nominalism as the default cultural mindset. I will not rehearse the details of this development here.[10] Suffice it to say that nominalism is not just an epistemological claim (that all our knowledge is knowledge of particular or unique objects) but also an ontological claim (that universals don't truly exist but are merely *nomina* or names that we subjectively assign). When nominalists explain why certain objects appear similar enough that we can categorize all of them as *people* or as *dogs*, they have recourse either to the divine will or to a strictly mechanical account (such as evolutionary biology). Nominalism, therefore, naturally tends to shade into mechanistic and materialist views. These in turn typically entail relativism and skepticism: it is difficult to assert moral and epistemological certainties if the world we see around us has no metaphysical or theological grounding. The five characteristics of Ur-Platonism tend to stand or fall together.

There is every reason, therefore, to home in on the key question of realism versus nominalism when we discuss metaphysics. Many contemporary biblical scholars reject realism in favor of nominalism because the latter dovetails perfectly with a historicism that focuses on the individual, unique character of historical events and tends to explain them mechanistically: methodological naturalism continues to be a common mode of exegesis, not only among historical critics but also among more traditional grammatical-historical scholars.[11]

---

[9]See Gerson's description in *From Plato to Platonism*, 12-13.

[10]For detailed discussion, see Louis Dupré, *Passage to Modernity: An Essay in the Hermeneutics of Nature and Culture* (New Haven, CT: Yale University Press, 1993), 3 and throughout; Michael Allen Gillespie, *The Theological Origins of Modernity* (Chicago: University of Chicago Press, 2008), 19-43; Thomas Pfau, *Minding the Modern: Human Agency, Intellectual Traditions, and Responsible Knowledge* (Notre Dame, IN: University of Notre Dame Press, 2013), 160-82.

[11]See the discussion in C. Stephen Evans, "Methodological Naturalism in Historical Biblical Scholarship," in *Jesus and the Restoration of Israel: A Critical Assessment of N. T. Wright's Jesus and the Victory of God*, ed. Carey C. Newman (Downers Grove, IL: InterVarsity Press, 1999), 180-205.

Nominalism, by bracketing and sometimes even excluding divine providence from the exegetical enterprise, yields a hermeneutic that is, in principle, strictly secular. There is no denying that a *pura scriptura* approach surreptitiously smuggles in a metaphysic that is grounded in the modern notion of *pura natura* and as such runs contrary to basic Christian convictions.

It should be clear why a non-metaphysical hermeneutic is not only undesirable but also impossible. Gerson's description of Ur-Platonism makes clear that one either adopts its various characteristics together or rejects them entirely. Rejecting them is not an elimination of metaphysics; it is the adoption of a different kind of metaphysic. We should not pretend, therefore, that we have to choose between taking either metaphysics or Christology as our starting point for our biblical and theological endeavors. Certainly, it is true that Christ is our hermeneutic starting point in the way that Plato (and metaphysics in general) can never be. After all, as I have insisted, we do not want an alien metaphysic that we subsequently impose on our reading of Scripture. The question, however, is *what kind* of metaphysic is most suitable to facilitate Christian exegesis and theology. Some types of metaphysics are more compatible with orthodox Christian commitments than others.

METAPHYSICS AND THE *SHEMA YISRAEL*

Metaphysical discourse has played a role in theology throughout the Christian tradition. This is perhaps most obviously the case in the Nicene confession of Christ as being of the same substance (*homoousion*) with the Father. Nicaea is one of the clearest examples of what its detractors call the "Hellenization" of Christianity and is often regarded with suspicion among those who are wary of the early church's departure from the concrete, Hebraic world and the alleged assimilation to the Greek philosophical environment. I believe the opposite to be the case: Christian Platonism helps solve the crisis of language surrounding the church's trinitarian formulations. The term *homoousion* is one of the most significant instances of Christian Platonism enabling us to make sense of the development of orthodox trinitarian thought.

I will focus on the shift from the Hebrew Shema to the Greek *homoousion* an example of so-called Hellenization. The Shema Yisrael was the basic Jewish confession of monotheism: "Hear, O Israel (*shema yisrael*): The LORD our God, the LORD is one" (Deut 6:4). The development from the Deuteronomic Shema to the Nicene *homoousion* may seem like a startling, perhaps illegitimate development from a particular, personal, Hebrew confession of faith in Yahweh as the only God to an abstract, metaphysical, Greek concept of God that places the Son on the same metaphysical level as the Father. Indeed, Jaroslav Pelikan, whose well-known book *Credo* traces the development of Christian creeds, observes that this development from Shema to *homoousion* is "the most radical and the most far-reaching case of successful creedal indigenization-cum-differentiation in a new culture during all of Christian history, and the one that has served as a conscious or unconscious paradigm for all the others."[12] As such, we have a helpful example of how metaphysics developed within Nicene Christianity.

The allegedly Hellenized metaphysic of the creed is not without biblical backing. Pelikan points out that the Nicene Creed, first adopted in the year 325, borrows some its key terminology from the Shema: "We believe in one God (*hena theon*)," and in "one Lord (*hena kyrion*) Jesus Christ," who is then declared to be "true God from true God" (*theon alēthinon ek theou alēthinou*). The language of God (*theos*) and Lord (*kyrios*) is the same as that used earlier in the Shema. Moreover, in adopting this language the creed is in sync also with Saint Paul's famous high christological pronouncement of 1 Corinthians 8:6, where he adapts the Shema to include Christ in its description of God: "For us there is one God (*heis theos*), the Father,

---

[12]Jaroslav Pelikan, *Credo: Historical and Theological Guide to Creeds and Confessions of Faith in the Christian Tradition* (New Haven, CT: Yale University Press, 2003), 330-31.

from whom are all things and for whom we exist, and one Lord (*heis kyrios*), Jesus Christ." Saint Paul takes the language of the Shema (*theos*, "God," and *kyrios*, "Lord") and applies the two terms to the Father and the Son respectively—without in any way detracting from Deuteronomic monotheism. Despite the differentiation between Father and Son, there is one God. The Nicene Creed follows the Pauline differentiation between God and Lord and also continues to confess the oneness of God: Christ the Lord is "true God from true God" and of the same substance as the Father (*homoousion tō patri*). Seeing as it continues the trajectory from the Shema via the Pauline confession of 1 Corinthians 8:6, Nicaea obviously desired to be biblical; the Nicene Creed does not impose an alien, nontheological metaphysic onto the Scriptures.

Despite the identical language, Paul's appropriation of the Shema does, of course, introduce a change. The difference between the Shema and the Nicene Creed is, as Pelikan observes, that the former concentrates on history, placing us squarely in the particularity of the exodus event and of the conquest of the Promised Land, while the *homoousion* focuses on ontology, offering us a theory of being in the context of trinitarian theology.[13] When the creed says that the Son is of "one substance with the Father" (*homoousion tō patri*), it does two things: it introduces the Greek term *homoousion* and it moves from a historical description to an ontological one.[14]

Those who would like to shield biblical interpretation from metaphysics are likely to question the legitimacy of this development. Still, it hardly amounts to a radical transformation or substitution. The advance from the Shema via Saint Paul's confession in 1 Corinthians 8:6 to the *homoousion* of the Nicene Creed is marked by a great deal of continuity. Moreover, Nicaea didn't initiate metaphysics: Paul's

---

[13]Pelikan, *Credo*, 333.

[14]To be sure, the Shema's assertion of divine oneness may well be said also to be ontological in character: the notion that only Yahweh is God is a metaphysical or ontological claim. Nonetheless, it is one that is tethered much more closely to history than is the Nicene Creed.

christological reconfiguration of the Shema already implies meta-physical speculation on the relationship between the Father and the Son. Nicaea's introduction of the *homoousion* is not out of line with Saint Paul's own articulation of the Father-Son relationship. As for those who insist on delimiting theological discourse to language that is purely biblical, they should perhaps be reminded that the Arians in the fourth century were the first to object that *homoousion* isn't a biblical term.[15] And, indeed, the term *ousia*, much like the English word *Trinity*, is not a biblical term.[16] But there is no reason why the mere absence of biblical terminology should make us shy away from the term *ousia*. It remains true that the classical doctrine of the Trinity is grounded in a metaphysic that is biblical and theological in its contours.

UNIVERSALS AND THE TRINITY

Biblical scholars often retort by asking the question: But is *ousia* language indispensable? Do we absolutely require the *homoousion* for orthodox Christianity? Strictly speaking, no. The term *ousia* is not itself enshrined as doctrine; only the reality to which it refers is the essence of the faith.[17] (Though, of course, words and concepts are closely linked, and a change in words usually implies at least some change also in doctrine.) Granted, we're not bound to words; we're

---

[15]Pelikan observes that the creed of the fourth Synod of Sirmium (359) objected to the term *ousia* on the grounds that "it gives offense as being unknown to the people, because it is not contained in the Scriptures." *Credo*, 334.

[16]Nonetheless, the term *ousia* derives from the verb *eimi* (to be), and so Pelikan rightly explains that the famous divine appellation of Ex 3:14 (*ego eimi ho ōn*) has been taken by much of the Christian tradition to be Mosaic endorsement of the term *ousia* and indirectly of the Nicene *homoousios*. *Credo*, 334-35.

[17]Pope John XXIII made a similar distinction in his opening words for the Second Vatican Council: "The substance of the ancient doctrine of the deposit of faith is one thing, and the way in which it is presented is another. And it is the latter that must be taken into great consideration with patience if necessary, everything being measured in the forms and proportions of a magisterium which is predominantly pastoral in character." "Pope John's Opening Speech to the Council," Vatican II—Voice of the Church, last modified November 24, 2019, http://vatican2voice.org/91docs/opening_speech.htm. See also Thomas G. Guarino, *Foundations of Systematic Theology* (New York: T&T Clark, 2005), 148-49.

bound to doctrines. But before we use this as an excuse to drop the term *ousia* and turn from metaphysics to a purely biblical theology, we may want to ask the question: What term will we use instead to say that the Son (1) is in some sense other than the Father; (2) is in no way inferior to the Father; and (3) is, in fact, in the very core of his being, the same as the Father? It was precisely to safeguard these three points that Nicaea embraced the term *homoousion*. The simple fact that it was rejected by the Arians who denied the Son's full and coequal divinity made it a suitable term for inclusion in the creed. The term *homoousion* may yet be the best term to safeguard the mystery of the Trinity. Historically, at least, metaphysics served in this instance to shore up the doctrine of the Trinity, and it is not clear how it is possible to do so without metaphysics.

The significance of metaphysics for trinitarian theology—and of the term *nature* (*ousia*) in particular—becomes clearer when we turn to Saint Gregory of Nyssa's *Letter to Ablabius* (or, as it is also known, his *On Not Three Gods*).[18] Gregory was convinced he needed a metaphysical framework in order to do justice both to monotheism and to its christological reconfiguration. Richard Hanson writes the following about the fourth-century development of trinitarian doctrine:

> The subjects under discussion between 318 and 381 were not, as has sometimes been alleged, those raised by Greek theology or philosophy and such as could only have been raised by people thinking in Greek terms. . . . In the fourth century there came to a head a crisis . . . which was not created by either Arius or Athanasius. It was the problem of how to reconcile two factors which were part of the very fabric of Christianity: monotheism, and the worship of Christ as divine. . . . The theologians of the

---

[18]Gregory of Nyssa, "Gregory of Nyssa's *Concerning We Should Think of Saying That There Are Not Three Gods* to Ablabius" (hereafter: *On Not Three Gods*), in *The Trinitarian Controversy*, trans. and ed. William G. Rusch (Philadelphia: Fortress, 1980), 149-61. See also the discussion in Lewis Ayres, *Nicaea and Its Legacy: An Approach to Fourth-Century Trinitarian Theology* (Oxford: Oxford University Press, 2004), 344-63.

Christian Church were slowly driven to a realization that the
deepest questions which face Christianity *cannot be answered
in purely biblical language, because the questions are about the
meaning of biblical language itself.* In the course of this search the
Church was impelled reluctantly to form dogma. It was the first
great and authentic example of the development of doctrine.[19]

Hanson's point is well made. We cannot limit Christian doctrine to
purely biblical language (*pura scriptura*) because this leaves open the
question of how we are to *understand* biblical discourse. We need
metaphysics to offer regulative guidelines and so to assist in the very
task of interpretation itself.

Gregory of Nyssa describes the dilemma of fourth-century theology already in the second paragraph of his *Letter to Ablabius*: "The
force of the inquiry necessarily brings one into one of two altogether
incompatible positions. One is according to common opinion: to say
that there are three gods, which is wicked. The other: not to bear
witness to the deity of the Son and the Spirit, which is ungodly and
absurd."[20] Gregory struggles here with the dilemma of maintaining
both the Deuteronomic Shema and the confession of the divinity of
the Son and the Spirit.

In the process of this intellectual struggle, Gregory introduces
some significant metaphysical scaffolding. He presents an intricate
discussion about universals and particulars. Saint Gregory faced the
objection: If Father, Son, and Spirit are coequal, each of them fully
divine, don't we end up with three gods? Isn't this polytheism?
Gregory had likely opened himself up to this criticism by comparing
the persons of the Trinity to three human persons, such as Peter,
James, and John. Just as they share one universal humanity while

---

[19]R. P. C. Hanson, *The Search for the Christian Doctrine of God: The Arian Controversy 318–381* (Edinburgh: T&T Clark, 1988), xx-xxi; emphasis added. See also Christopher A. Hall, *Learning Theology with the Church Fathers* (Downers Grove, IL: InterVarsity Press, 2002), 55.
[20]Gregory of Nyssa, *On Not Three Gods*, 149.

they're nonetheless distinct, so also in the Trinity, there is a common divinity, and yet three divine persons. Gregory's analogy might seem to veer dangerously close to tritheism.[21]

To counter the objection, Gregory makes use of one of the characteristics of Ur-Platonism, namely, its antinominalism. He insists that we must distinguish between that which is common within a group and that which is unique to a particular subject. He introduces the general term *mankind* or *humanity* (*anthrōpotēs*) and points out that people use the word *man* (*anthrōpos*) both in a general sense for what is common to all people (just as we still do with the word *humanity*) *and* for individual human beings such as Luke and Stephan.[22] Now, Gregory makes a fascinating move here. He claims that properly speaking, we really should restrict the term *man* to our common humanity—in other words, it properly refers to a universal. It's only by an "abuse of language," insists Gregory, that we talk about "many men." To talk about "many men" is like saying there are "many human natures."[23] And while Gregory isn't overly bothered by the confusion between *man* (as a universal) and *man* (as a particular) he *does* believe that something crucial is at stake when we apply the word *god* not just to the common divinity of the three persons, but also to each of them individually. Strictly speaking, even talk of three men is already erroneous, though Gregory is willing to tolerate such language. But talk of three gods isn't just erroneous; for when it comes to divine doctrine, "'minor' points are not minor," cautions Gregory.[24]

So, Gregory distinguishes between particulars and the universals ("Forms" or "Ideas") in which individual or particular objects participate, and he applies the distinction to God: we speak of one God

---

[21]This, of course, is an objection today's social trinitarians also face. Unlike Gregory (to whom they sometimes erroneously appeal), they don't deflect this criticism by highlighting the divine unity.

[22]Gregory of Nyssa, *On Not Three Gods*, 151.

[23]Gregory of Nyssa, *On Not Three Gods*, 150.

[24]Gregory of Nyssa, *On Not Three Gods*, 151.

and of one *ousia* or nature (the divine universal, as it were), while maintaining that there are three *hypostases* or persons (the particulars, as it were). Just as it is eminently rational (within a Platonist metaphysic) to say that three human persons share a common nature, so Nyssen sees nothing problematic about suggesting that three divine *hypostases* share a common *ousia*.

To be sure, one may question whether this distinction between universals and particulars is as helpful as it may seem. The three divine persons (*hypostases*) may share a common nature (*ousia*), but don't we say of each of them that he is divine? Gregory's objection to the language of *man* as referring to an individual cannot hide the fact that each individual human being has its own, distinct center of consciousness, with its own faculties of intellect and will and with its own, distinct set of actions. If we apply this to God, do we not still have polytheism of a sort? (As an aside, to my mind this is an important objection, and it is the Achilles heel of social trinitarianism, which often has difficulty avoiding the pitfall of tritheism.)

Saint Gregory makes clear, however, that the unity of the three divine persons is much stronger than unity among human persons. The analogy between the common humanity of Peter, James, and John, on the one hand, and the common divinity of Father, Son, and Spirit, on the other hand, breaks down, says Gregory, at a crucial point. Peter, James, and John all make their own decisions and undertake their own actions. This kind of distinctiveness does not apply to the Trinity. It is not as though the Father does one thing, the Son another, and the Spirit yet another. Rather, explains Gregory, "every activity which pervades from God to creation and is named according to our manifold designs starts off from the Father, proceeds through the Son, and is completed by the Holy Spirit."[25] This theological principle has become known in Latin as the idea that *opera trinitatis ad extra indivisa sunt* (the external activities of the Trinity are indivisible).

---

[25]Gregory of Nyssa, *On Not Three Gods*, 155.

It is with good reason that Gregory's book is called *On Not Three Gods*. Gregory sets out in this book to highlight the unity of God rather than the distinctness of the persons: he wants to counter the objection that his human analogy (Peter, James, and John) implies polytheism. To this end, he first applies the distinction between universals and particulars to the doctrine of the Trinity and then adds that even the unity among the divine persons runs much deeper than that among human persons. John Behr rightly summarizes Gregory of Nyssa's thought by saying, "There is one God, and one divinity, because there is one 'transcendent power,' the Father, who works by the Son and in the Spirit, not as three people cooperating together in fellowship, but in terms for which there is no adequate analogy in the created world."[26] Gregory's participatory ontology—with particulars participating in universals—allows him to maintain both the distinctness of the divine persons and their sameness in terms of their divine nature (*ousia*). By contrast, when we reject Saint Gregory's Ur-Platonism and adopt a nominalist metaphysic, we invariably end up with a social trinitarianism in which it is typically unclear how the three persons are truly one.[27] To Gregory, it seemed clear that biblical orthodoxy required him to adopt a Platonic metaphysic.

PARTICIPATION IN CHRIST

On a Pauline understanding, we are saved by being "in Christ" (*en Christō*). Whatever else we may want to say about how soteriology functions biblically, our salvation is grounded in the truth that as human beings we are included in Christ. This acknowledgment is, of course, not unique to theologians. Biblical scholars too recognize the

---

[26]John Behr, *The Nicene Faith*, vol. 2 of *The Formation of Christian Theology* (Crestwood, NY: St. Vladimir's Seminary Press, 2001), 435; see also 420-21, 425-26.

[27]Social trinitarianism comes close to lapsing into tritheism when it advocates three centers of consciousness in God. See, for instance, Jürgen Moltmann, *The Trinity and the Kingdom* (1981; repr., Minneapolis: Fortress, 1993); Catherine Mowry LaCugna, *God for Us: The Trinity and Christian Life* (San Francisco: HarperSanFrancisco, 1991).

centrality of this participatory language in Paul's letters. There may be discussion among biblical theologians as to whether justification or participation is the dominating motif of Saint Paul's overall theology,[28] but it would be impossible simply to ignore the latter. (On my understanding, participation is the more central category, as I think it undergirds justification.) The question I want to raise here, therefore, is not whether participation language appears in Saint Paul's letters but whether we need a particular metaphysic to make sense of a participatory soteriology. I hope to make clear that a nominalist metaphysic, which continues to be the (often unacknowledged) go-to approach of much biblical scholarship, cannot account for Saint Paul's participatory soteriology. The apostle's theology operates with a metaphysic in which we are *ontologically linked together* and in which we *genuinely become one new humanity,* and it is only a realist metaphysic that is able to do justice to this.

Already in Saint Irenaeus in the late second century, participation functioned as the central category for soteriology. As we saw in the previous chapter, Irenaeus speaks mostly of recapitulation (*anakephalaiōsis*), a term he adopts from Ephesians 1:10 (which states that God aims to "unite [*anakephalaiōsthai*] all things in him, things in heaven and things on earth"). On Irenaeus's understanding, Christ is the head (*caput* in Latin, *kephalē* in Greek) of the new humanity. Irenaeus did not mean to say that the head (Christ) is one thing, and the body (the new humanity) another. Such an *external* or *nominal* connection between Christ and humanity would not do justice to the intimacy of the relationship. Rather, Irenaeus understood the biblical narrative to imply a *participatory* or *real* connection between

---

[28]The traditional Protestant view held that justification is the heart of Pauline theology. In the wake of Albert Schweitzer's theology, New Perspective adherents (as well as others) have argued instead that participation is the primary key to Paul's theology. For the latter view, see, e.g., James D. G. Dunn, *The Theology of Paul the Apostle* (Grand Rapids, MI: Eerdmans, 1998), 390-412; Michael Gorman, *Becoming the Gospel: Paul, Participation, and Mission* (Grand Rapids, MI: Eerdmans, 2015); Garwood P. Anderson, *Paul's New Perspective: Charting a Soteriological Journey* (Downers Grove, IL: IVP Academic, 2016), 384-97.

Christ and those he represents. For Irenaeus, Christ's life and work are salvific because we are actually or ontologically included in who he is and what he does.

It may be worthwhile to unpack this in a bit more detail because the Irenaean perspective of recapitulation—his participatory soteriology—has laid the groundwork for subsequent patristic soteriology both East and West. It is perhaps easiest to explain Irenaeus's approach with reference to three specific biblical passages in addition to Ephesians 1:10. The first is Matthew 4:1-11, which relates Christ's temptation by the devil in the wilderness. Irenaeus begins his discussion of this passage in book 5.21 of *Against Heresies* with the following comment: Christ "in His work of recapitulation, summed up all things (*omnia recapitulans recapitulatus est*), both waging war against our enemy, and crushing him who had at the beginning led us away captives in Adam."[29] It is Christ's obedient resistance to temptation that constitutes his faithful recapitulation of Adamic life and so the reversal of the fate of Adam's race.

Irenaeus explains in some detail how this recapitulation functioned.[30] Christ resisted Satan's first temptation of turning stone into bread by quoting Deuteronomy 8:3: "Man shall not live by bread alone" (Mt 4:4). The bishop of Lyons comments: "The corruption of man, therefore, which occurred in paradise by both [of our first parents] eating, was done away with by [the Lord's] want of food in this world."[31] Irenaeus posits a typological connection between Adam's temptation by means of food and Christ's temptation by the same. Salvation lies in the fact that unlike Adam, Christ did not give in to this temptation. Next, Irenaeus turns to the second temptation, namely, to throw himself down from the pinnacle of the temple. Here Irenaeus argues that it is Christ's obedient humility (in adhering to

---

[29]Irenaeus, *Against Heresies* 5.21.1 (*ANF* 1:548).
[30]See D. Jeffrey Bingham, *Irenaeus' Use of Matthew's Gospel in Adversus Haereses*, TEG 7 (Leuven: Peeters, 1998), 274-81.
[31]Irenaeus, *Against Heresies* 5.21.2 (*ANF* 1:549); square brackets in *ANF*.

the law's injunction in Deuteronomy 6:16 not to put God to the test) that defeats the serpent's "pride of reason."[32] When Satan finally directly asks Jesus to worship him, Jesus exposes Satan's identity as the great apostate and, intimates Irenaeus, conquers him by being faithful to the law. Irenaeus puts it this way: "And thus, vanquishing him for the third time, He spurned him from Him finally as being conquered out of the law; and there was done away with that infringement of God's commandment which had occurred in Adam, by means of the precept of the law, which the Son of man observed, who did not transgress the commandment of God."[33] For Irenaeus, where Adam caved to temptation, Jesus was faithful, thus yielding salvation.

Irenaeus detects the same kind of typological link between Adam and Christ in Romans 5:12 and 1 Corinthians 15:21-22.[34] Taking his cue from Saint Paul's distinction between the first and the second Adam, Irenaeus treats Adam as a type or figure of Christ.[35] In this way he ties recapitulation to the restoration of humanity in three ways.[36] First, he maintains that the *birth* of Christ recapitulates the creation of Adam: as Adam was created "from untilled and as yet virgin soil," so did also the Word, "recapitulating Adam in Himself, rightly receive a birth, enabling Him to gather up Adam [into Himself], from Mary, who was as yet a virgin."[37] Christ's birth from Mary is thus a recapitulation of the creation of Adam.

Second, Irenaeus highlights the *obedience* of Christ in the face of temptation. It was necessary for the Son of God truly to become the

---

[32]Irenaeus, *Against Heresies* 5.21.2 (*ANF* 1:549).

[33]Irenaeus, *Against Heresies* 5.21.2 (*ANF* 1:549-50).

[34]The rest of this paragraph is taken from Hans Boersma, "Justification Within Recapitulation: Irenaeus in Ecumenical Dialogue," *IJST* 22 (2020): 169-90.

[35]Irenaeus, *Against Heresies* 3.18.2 (*ANF* 1:446); 3.18.7 (*ANF* 1:448); 3.21.10 (*ANF* 1:454); 5.16.3 (*ANF* 1:544). See also Ben C. Blackwell, "Paul and Irenaeus," in *Paul and the Second Century: The Legacy of Paul's Life, Letters, and Teaching*, ed. Michael F. Bird and Joseph R. Dodson, LNTS 412 (London: T&T Clark, 2011), 201.

[36]I discuss Christ's recapitulation as the second Adam in greater detail in "Redemptive Hospitality in Irenaeus: A Model for Ecumenicity in a Violent World," *ProEccl* 11 (2002): 216-19.

[37]Irenaeus, *Against Heresies* 3.21.10 (*ANF* 1:454); square brackets in *ANF*.

Son of Man, insists Irenaeus, for "unless man had overcome the enemy of man, the enemy would not have been legitimately vanquished."[38] As we have already seen, three times Jesus quoted the law against the adversary's temptation, which on Irenaeus's view means his obedience checked and reversed Adam's disobedience.

Third, Irenaeus also includes Christ's *suffering and death* within the purview of his theory of recapitulation. The bishop expresses this perhaps most poignantly when he comments, "And the sin that was wrought through the tree was undone by the obedience of the tree, obedience to God whereby the Son of man was nailed to the tree."[39] Christ's obedient suffering and death on the cross cancel out Adam's disobedience in paradise.

For Irenaeus recapitulation truly works soteriologically (and, likewise, typology truly works hermeneutically) because Christ is the archetype who includes in himself all of Adamic existence. This is where the second question mentioned in the introduction comes into play: Why, still today, should we have recourse to a *Platonic* metaphysic? Why not turn to a different metaphysic that is more suitable to our own cultural context? One basic reason is this: it is a Platonic metaphysic that allows us to make sense of the language of Christ as archetype. As the new Adam or the new humanity, Christ includes all of humanity, so that when he faithfully retraces its origin, life, and death, he renews and saves it. By implication, Irenaeus was an Ur-Platonist. The degree to which Irenaeus consciously built on Plato remains somewhat unclear.[40] At the very least, the bishop of Lyons subconsciously adopted, presumably by way of his predecessor Justin Martyr, a Platonic understanding of the relationship between

---

[38]Irenaeus, *Against Heresies* 3.18.7 (*ANF* 1:549-50).

[39]Irenaeus, *Proof of the Apostolic Preaching*, ed. and trans. Joseph P. Smith, ACW 16 (New York: Paulist Press, 1952), par. 34 (p. 69). Irenaeus also uses the typology of the tree in *Against Heresies* 5.16.3 (*ANF* 1:544); 5.17.3-4 (*ANF* 1:545-46); 5.19.1 (*ANF* 1:547).

[40]Anthony Briggman shows that in several places Irenaeus directly appeals to Plato's writings. "Revisiting Irenaeus' Philosophical Acumen," *VC* 65 (2011): 115-24.

particulars and universals—in this case, particular human beings and the humanity of Christ. Eric Osborn rightly maintains, therefore, that Irenaeus worked with a "Platonic paradigm," in which creaturely objects participate in Platonic Forms.[41] Irenaeus's inclusive or participatory soteriology presupposes that our humanity is included in that of Christ. Because it does so, our human nature has a participatory or real connection with Christ's humanity: it is saved in and through his recapitulation.

Irenaeus's antinominalist or realist understanding of human nature, along with its participatory understanding of salvation, may be traced throughout the church fathers and the subsequent tradition. Consistently, the theological metaphysic at work is one in which our human nature is healed (and transfigured) by participating in the new humanity of Christ. Put differently, it is only because Christ's human nature is inclusive in character—functioning, as it were, as a Platonic Form—that our humanity is redeemed, restored, and divinized. The main difference between Christ's human nature and ours, according to Chalcedonian Christology—famously articulated by the sixth-century monk Leontius of Byzantium—is that our human nature is hypostatic or personal, while Christ's human nature is anhypostatic or impersonal. That is to say, Christ's humanity has no subsistence or individuality apart from the eternal Word of God. ·Christ's human nature, therefore, has no personality or hypostasis of its own.[42] His is a common or universal human nature.

Contemporary biblical scholarship, particularly the kind that focuses on quests for the historical Jesus, takes its starting point not in the divine person of the Word (in which the human nature of Christ traditionally was thought to subsist) but in the human person of Jesus,

---

[41]Eric Osborn, *Irenaeus of Lyons* (Cambridge: Cambridge University Press, 2004), 15-16.
[42]See the excellent retrieval of this Chalcedonian approach by Aaron Riches, *Ecce Homo: On the Divine Unity of Christ* (Grand Rapids, MI: Eerdmans, 2016).

who then may perhaps also be thought to be divine. The implications of this reversal are significant, as David Brown makes clear:

> It is often forgotten that for most of Christian history Christ was envisaged as bearing only a universal humanity, with all personhood and characterization provided by his divine nature. In theory, therefore, when stress moved to the humanity, this should have brought a universal type of humanity, easily applicable to each and every one of us, whereas what in fact happened was the discovery that the incarnation had entailed precisely the same sort of particularity to which we are all subject. It looks, therefore, as though, whereas prior to the modern period Christ's universal humanity was the pattern towards which the particulars of the lives of the saints were made to conform, now the only way for us to generate an analogous relationship is by comparing one particular, the life of Jesus, with that of other such particulars.[43]

Historical Jesus research does not typically entertain the notion of a universal humanity of Christ. The reason is the prior metaphysical nominalist stance of every one of the quests for the historical Jesus. The earlier tradition, however, beginning with Irenaeus's articulation of recapitulation, took its starting point in Ur-Platonism.

My purpose is not simply to point up the difference between premodern and modern ways of reading the Gospels and of understanding the personhood of Christ—though this is significant in itself since it illustrates how a change in metaphysics demands a change in our reading of Scripture. I aim more deeply than this. The point is that we cannot do justice to the Pauline *en Christō* without the antinominalist metaphysic of the patristic and medieval eras. What could it possibly mean to be "in Christ" on the assumption that the human

---

[43]David Brown, *Discipleship and Imagination: Christian Tradition and Truth* (Oxford: Oxford University Press, 2000), 81.

Jesus is his own person and that we are persons ontologically separate from him? Biblical scholars are typically forced to downplay the import of Paul's language of participation by explaining it as a metaphor that speaks of some kind of external or nominal relationship. E. P. Sanders, for example, is at a loss how properly to understand the language of participation: "What does this mean? How are we to understand it? We seem to lack a category of 'reality'—real participation in Christ, real possession of the Spirit—which lies between naive cosmological speculation and belief in magical transference on the one hand and a revised self-understanding on the other. I must confess that I do not have a new category of perception to propose here."[44] One could envision a variety of responses to Sanders, different ways of explaining participation in Christ.[45] Many of these would fall short of genuine, ontological realism.[46] Sanders himself explicitly speaks of "real participation." Metaphysically, however, the options are limited: one either commits to realism or to nominalism. If it is truly "real participation" that we are after, we must opt for Christian Platonism. Only a realist metaphysic can robustly claim that human beings are saved through a participatory or real sharing in Christ.

CONCLUSION

We should be suspicious of *pura scriptura* approaches to biblical scholarship that claim to disavow metaphysics. Such claims regularly caution against imposing an alien metaphysic onto the Scriptures. The caution itself is salutary enough. As I have tried to show in this

---

[44]E. P. Sanders, *Paul and Palestinian Judaism: A Comparison of Patterns of Religion*, 40th anniversary ed. (Minneapolis: Fortress, 2017), 522.

[45]See, for instance, Michael J. Thate, Kevin J. Vanhoozer, and Constantine R. Campbell, eds., *"In Christ" in Paul: Explorations in Paul's Theology of Union and Participation* (Grand Rapids, MI: Eerdmans, 2018).

[46]Richard Hays is a fine exception. He hints: "My own guess is that Sanders's insights would be supported and clarified by careful study of participation motifs in patristic theology, particularly the thought of the Eastern fathers." *The Faith of Jesus Christ: The Narrative Substructure of Galatians 3:11–4:11*, 2nd ed. (Grand Rapids, MI: Eerdmans, 2002), xxxii.

chapter, however, both in terms of trinitarian theology and in terms of Christology, the church fathers drew on Platonism for theological reasons. Their Ur-Platonism was not an uncritical embrace of the Platonic tradition but was rather a turn to aspects of Plato that they were convinced facilitated a proper articulation of Christian truth claims. It is in this sense that the Platonism of the Fathers and medieval theologians was *Christian* Platonism. They selectively drew on the philosophical tradition in order to articulate a distinctly theological metaphysic, and they recognized the truth of the dictum in the title of this chapter: no Plato, no Scripture. We need a good dose of Plato for some of the key teachings of Scripture to become intelligible.

It is not as though the danger of an alien interpolation of metaphysics is illusory. We witness this danger when people suggest that because each and every age has its own philosophies and metaphysics, we should try to find cultural points of context wherever possible. The reason most of the tradition has been Christian Platonist is not that the cultural context made it the most congenial option but that Christian Platonism is more suitable than most other metaphysics in supporting the teaching of Scripture. Pope Benedict XVI put it well in his famous 2006 Regensburg lecture: "The encounter between the Biblical message and Greek thought did not happen by chance. The vision of Saint Paul, who saw the roads to Asia barred and in a dream saw a Macedonian man plead with him: 'Come over to Macedonia and help us!' (cf. *Acts* 16:6-10)—this vision can be interpreted as a 'distillation' of the intrinsic necessity of a rapprochement between Biblical faith and Greek inquiry."[47] In articulating the Christian faith, our task is not to bring together the pure, biblical teaching with the philosophies or metaphysics of the day. Rather, the theological heritage of Christian Platonism is the received tradition on which it is

---

[47]See "Faith, Reason and the University: Memories and Reflections," Libreria Editrice Vaticana, 2006, www.vatican.va/holy_father/benedict_xvi/speeches/2006/september /documents/hf_ben-xvi_spe_20060912_university-regensburg_en.html.

irresponsible to renege and on which we should continue to build under new circumstances.

Ironically, those who treat biblical scholarship as primarily a historical discipline are most susceptible to the danger of introducing an alien metaphysic. Whenever they treat exegesis as a matter of *pura scriptura*, the temptation will be to bring it into harmony with the metaphysic of the day, unaware that they are the ones importing an alien metaphysic. Much like Alisdair MacIntyre's insistence that our first task in debate with Enlightenment philosophy is to dispute its claim to neutrality and to point out that instead it is a tradition of its own, so our first task in dialogue with contemporary biblical scholarship is to dispute its theological neutrality and to point out its metaphysical starting points.[48] My overall plea in this chapter, therefore, is for biblical scholars to reflect on the metaphysic that (often unawares) they presuppose and often import into their interpretive endeavors. Given the inescapability of exegesis engaging in metaphysics, it is imperative that we consistently question its congruity with the gospel. No Plato, no Scripture.

---

[48]See Alisdair MacIntyre, *Whose Justice? Which Rationality?* (Notre Dame, IN: University of Notre Dame Press, 1988), 396-99.

NO PROVIDENCE, NO SCRIPTURE

VARIETIES OF SPEECH

God comes to us in biblical words on which we are meant to stake our lives.

But why take such a risk? Does it make sense to stake one's life on words? This chapter argues that we are justified in doing so inasmuch as the words of Scripture are uniquely caught up in divine providence. God uses human words to make known his will. These human words become divine Scripture by participating in a profound, dynamic manner in divine providence. This same participation of scriptural words in God's eternal providence explains why we interpret them in a certain mode, namely, with a view to our spiritual maturation and ultimately our eternal salvation. In short, both the character of these words as Scripture and our reading of them in light of our heavenly future are dependent on God's providence: no providence, no Scripture.

Biblical scholarship since the seventeenth century has increasingly cut this link between providence and Scripture, and as a result has come to ignore both the divine character of Scripture's human words and the need to read them primarily with spiritual intent. This chapter, then, will highlight the importance of providence for the way we read Scripture. *And so, the third thing that I, as a theologian, wish biblical scholars knew is that their work benefits from the recognition that in God's providence the Scriptures are unlike any other book.*

It is not only Scripture that is taken up in divine providence. All of creation is providentially structured. God is present everywhere and as such provides everywhere (see Ps 139:7-10; Acts 17:28). A sacramental ontology—a metaphysic that maintains that God is present throughout creation—implies a high view of divine providence. God's presence in all that he has made ought to give us basic trust in the goodness and the purposiveness of life. God provides, and his very presence guarantees that human existence is not absurd but ordered. Through the Spirit, God draws us ever more deeply into Christ and so to our appointed end in the beatific vision. Theologians sometimes refer to this as "general providence," a phrase that is useful as long as we remember that also this so-called *general* providence aims at the ultimate telos of seeing God face to face. Whatever God does in creation aims at the transfiguration of his people along with the rest of the created order.

Just as we shouldn't separate nature and the supernatural into two separate compartments, so we should avoid separating general and special providence, as well as inspired and noninspired books. God speaks everywhere. Despite the absence of speech, words, and voice (Ps 19:3), the heavens "declare" (*safar*) the glory of God and the sky "proclaims" (*nagad*) his handiwork (Ps 19:1). Seven times Psalm 29 insists that the "voice of the LORD" (*qol yahweh*) thunders over the waters, flashing forth flames of fire, breaking trees, causing earthquakes, and triggering labor pangs among deer. This same "word" (*davar*) of God that instigates weather changes (Ps 147:15, 18) serves as a synonym for the "statutes" (*khuqqim*) and "rules" (*mishpatim*) that God has given to Israel (Ps 147:19-20). Whenever God speaks, he speaks his mind. All God's speech—whether through the created order more broadly or through commandments for his people—is part of the economic mission of the Son and is anchored in the eternal mission or generation of the Son from the Father. Whenever God speaks, he shows his true colors, and for that reason every providential act in history ultimately has a salvific aim.

God's speech is nonetheless multifarious in character. Most obviously, even though nature and the supernatural cannot be separated, biblical language often distinguishes them. The Psalms for example note a difference between God's presence and speech in nature and in the law. The words, "The heavens declare the glory of God" of Psalm 19:1 introduce the first half of the psalm, celebrating God's work in creation. The second part of the psalm praises the law: "The law of the LORD is perfect, reviving the soul" (Ps 19:7). The distinction serves to highlight Israel's privilege as God's elect nation: Israel receives the law from the Creator of the universe. Psalm 147 similarly distinguishes between God's voice in nature and in Israel. On the one hand, God's glory is legible for everyone to read in the stars, clouds, grass, beasts, and birds, as well as in snow, frost, and ice. On the other hand, the Lord "builds up Jerusalem" (Ps 147:2), "strengthens the bars of your gates" (Ps 147:13), and in the giving of his law "has not dealt thus with any other nation" (Ps 147:20). The reason this song begins and ends with the words, "Praise the LORD" (Ps 147:1, 20) is that the God of all creation has a "preferential option" for Jerusalem, Zion, Jacob, Israel, the outcasts, the broken-hearted, the humble, and the God fearers (Ps 147:2-3, 6, 11-12, 19). Psalm 19 and Psalm 147 both make clear that when God speaks to Israel in the law, he makes himself present in a special way. God's law given to Israel reveals his providence in an incomparably rich manner (short of God's ultimate self-revelation in the incarnation). We should be sensitive to the variety of ways—and the variety of intensities—in which God appears to us.

The distinction between general and special revelation (which is by no means a separation) is one indication that God's speech takes on a variety of forms.

The variety of divine speech comes to the fore also within Scripture itself. Not every biblical text has an equally central place in divine providence. Just think of the prominent position in ancient Israel of the Torah compared to the Prophets and the Writings. Similarly, the twice-daily recitation of the Shema (Deut 6:4-9; 11:13-21; and Num 15:37-41) renders it the core of the Jewish faith. And Jesus makes clear that love of God and neighbor (as demanded in Deut 6:5 and Lev 19:18) is "the great commandment in the Law" (Mt 22:36). The four Gospels, too, are central in Christian liturgy in a way that no other biblical book is, while the Psalms (and often also the Song of Songs) have played the role of favorite throughout the history of monastic spirituality. To have a canon-in-the-canon does not mean that we have lost respect for other parts of the Bible; it is a recognition that sacramentality comes in degrees of intensity. Christianity is similar here to the Platonic tradition: what makes a Platonic hierarchy harmonic rather than oppressive is that the varying modes of participation in being all have their own, distinct tunes to play and so make for a polyphonic whole. All of creation and all of Scripture is theophanic—God appears in all of it and speaks in all of it. But he does not do this everywhere in the same manner or in the same intensity.

SCRIPTURE AS PROVIDENTIAL SACRAMENT IN ORIGEN

The third-century theologian Origen of Alexandria was keenly aware of the participatory link between this-worldly words and the eternal Word of God. To articulate this link, Origen relied in part on a Stoic notion of providence (*pronoia*). For the Stoics, providence was a rational logos-principle that indwells the natural world and gives it order and direction. From the right perspective, we can see how everything that happens, even something that may seem problematic or evil, has its proper place within the overall providential order.[1] Drawing on these Stoic notions, Origen could refer to the Word of God simply as providence (*pronoia*). For Origen, too, providence pervades everything that happens, so that everything ultimately serves God's good purposes.[2]

Origen believed, rightly I think, that the providential Logos makes himself present not only in the world in a general manner but also in particular ways in the Scriptures, in Jesus Christ, in the soul of the believer, and in the church.[3] Hans Urs von Balthasar mentions three of these four "incarnations" when he comments: "Incarnation in the scripture and in an individual body were both an image and means to the third incarnation which was the meaning and purpose of the redemption: the incarnation of the Logos in his mystical body."[4] The language of a fourfold "incarnation" may seem to elide any and all differences among the four. This is not the conclusion we should draw, and it is not what Origen intended. Jesus Christ is, to use a later term, the *Ursakrament*: the hypostatic union implies that the divine nature is fully present only in the one who is true God from true God. It is true, of course, that even in the incarnation itself, the divine presence often remained hidden apart from unique occasions such as the transfiguration, when the veil between time and eternity was temporarily

[1] See A. A. Long and D. N. Sedley, *The Hellenistic Philosophers*, vol. 1, *Translations of the Principal Sources with Philosophical Commentary* (Cambridge: Cambridge University Press, 1987), 323-33; Michael Graves, "The 'Pagan' Background of Patristic Exegetical Methods," in *Ancient Faith for the Church's Future*, ed. Mark Husbands and Jeffrey P. Greenman (Downers Grove, IL: IVP Academic, 2008), 103-4.

[2] As a Christian theologian, Origen did not go along with the Stoic notion of the Logos as a material principle that was part and parcel of creation (*Contra Celsum* 6.71), and Origen also treated free will as something compatible with providence (*Princ.* 3.3.5).

[3] See my discussion in Hans Boersma, *Scripture as Real Presence: Sacramental Exegesis in the Early Church* (Grand Rapids, MI: Baker Academic, 2019), 111-18. See also Henri de Lubac, *History and Spirit: The Understanding of Scripture According to Origen*, trans. Anne Englund Nash with Juvenal Merriell (San Francisco: Ignatius, 2007), 385-426.

[4] Hans Urs von Balthasar, ed., *Origen: Spirit and Fire—A Thematic Anthology of His Writings*, trans. Robert J. Daly (Washington, DC: Catholic University of America Press, 1984), 148.

lifted and the disciples were so transfigured that they saw the divine reality (*res*) of the sacrament of Christ.[5] The main point here is that in varying ways and to varying degrees God makes human realities participate in the eternal providential Word of God.[6] Or, put differently, human realities—first and foremost Christ's human body, but also the words of Scripture—can function as theophanies, carriers of the divine presence.

In his third homily on Genesis, Origen elaborates on the link between providence and human speech. Here he discusses Abraham's circumcision as described in Genesis 17.[7] Because God speaks to Abraham when he makes his covenant with the patriarch, Origen places the narrative in the context of divine speech: "We read in many passages of the divine Scripture that God speaks to men."[8] That God speaks does not mean, Origen clarifies, that God has a mouth and a tongue. We talk about God "speaking" because he makes known to us what is good for us. What we call God's speech, therefore, is a manifestation of his providence. Origen makes clear that God "cares (*curare*) about mortal affairs and . . . nothing happens in heaven or earth apart from his providence (*providentia*)."[9] Providence, he explains, is "that by which he attends to (*procurat*) and manages (*dispensat*) and makes provision (*providet*) for the things which happen."[10]

---

[5]Eastern and Western church fathers unanimously agreed that it was the *disciples* who were transfigured on the mountain: Christ's deity always already shone through in his humanity, and the miracle of the transfiguration was that the disciples were now able to discern this divine light. See John Anthony McGuckin, *The Transfiguration of Christ in Scripture and Tradition* (Lewiston, NY: Edwin Mellen, 1986).

[6]The Word of God functions for Origen like forms do for Plato in that for Origen the Word contains the eternal archetypes for created things (*Princ.* 1.4.5). However, Origen critiques Plato for the notion that forms would be independent of the Creator (*Princ.* 2.3.6). See Mark J. Edwards, "Origen," *The Stanford Encyclopedia of Philosophy*, Summer 2018 ed., ed. Edward N. Zalta, https://plato.stanford.edu/archives/sum2018/entries/origen.

[7]For the following paragraph I have benefited from Peter W. Martens, *Origen and Scripture: The Contours of the Exegetical Life* (Oxford: Oxford University Press, 2012), 195-96.

[8]Origen, *Homilies on Genesis and Exodus*, ed. Hermigild Dressler, trans. Ronald E. Heine, FC 71 (Washington, DC: Catholic University of America Press, 1982), 3.1 (89).

[9]Origen, *Homilies on Genesis* 3.2 (89).

[10]Origen, *Homilies on Genesis* 3.2 (89).

Inasmuch, then, as God wants to provide for us and care for us, he makes known his will to us:

> In accordance with this profession, therefore, that God is the provider (*provisorem*) and manager (*dispensatorem*) of all things, it follows that he makes known what he wishes or what is advantageous for men. For if he should not make these things known he will not be the provider (*provisor*) for man nor will he be believed to care for mortal affairs. Since, therefore, God makes known to men what he wishes them to do, in what particularly appropriate way is he to be said to make it known? Is it not by that one which is used and known by men?[11]

God makes known his desire to provide for us by a means that "is used and known by men," namely, speech. Surely, silence doesn't tell us anything about God's kind provision for us, and so we should instead be talking about God "speaking to us."[12] God's providence, in other words, comes to expression in his speech. Providence, for Origen, is the eternal framework or grounding for what we call God's words in history. Peter Martens comments that for Origen, "God's particular action in Scripture was the particular instance of God's larger providential action in the cosmos as a whole."[13] Words from God express his providential care for Abraham and for all of us.[14]

So, if God has no mouth or tongue, how does his providential Word reach us? God, says Origen, "either inspires the heart of each of the saints or causes the sound of a voice to reach his ears."[15] When God uses an actual sound, it is the sound of a unique kind, not produced by a tongue but "governed by the control of the will from

---

[11]Origen, *Homilies on Genesis* 3.2 (90).
[12]Origen, *Homilies on Genesis* 3.2 (90).
[13]Martens, *Origen and Scripture*, 195.
[14]See Mark W. Elliott's discussion on providence and Scripture in Origen in *Providence Perceived: Divine Action from a Human Point of View* (Berlin: de Gruyter, 2015), 17-18.
[15]Origen, *Homilies on Genesis* 3.2 (90).

above";[16] when there is no sound, the Spirit illumines someone's mind and directs it to speak. With or without voice, God makes known his providential will to the prophets and patriarchs: "And so, whether in this way or in that which we mentioned above, when God makes his will known he is said to have spoken."[17] Origen links God's prophetic speech to his will, which is to say, his providential care and provision for us.

Origen is essentially correct. Divine providence has implications both for our understanding of what Scripture is and for how we are supposed to read it. For Origen, providence implies that God uses human words to make known his will so as to lead us to salvation. This in turn suggests a close link between Scripture's words, on the one hand, and its providential grounding and salvific end, on the other hand. God's actions in history, as well as the words that Scripture uses to describe them, participate, according to Origen, in God's providential, salvific plan in Christ. Or, we could also say, Origen treats the biblical narrative as the salvific means linking eternal providence with eternal salvation. Scripture, for Origen, serves as a means of grace; it has a sacramental function. By implication, the task of the reader is to search Scripture for how it serves this sacramental role.

In *Homilies* 23 and 25 on the book of Joshua, Origen embarks on an extended conversation about providence in connection with the division of the Promised Land through the casting of lots in Joshua 17–19. He begins *Homily* 23 by drawing attention to Leviticus 16, where one lot is taken for God and the other for the scapegoat (Lev 16:8).[18] Next, Origen observes that Caleb had been assigned a share *not* by lot, but "according to the commandment of the Lord" (see Josh 14:13).[19] The tribes on the west side of the Jordan River, however,

---

[16]Origen, *Homilies on Genesis* 3.2 (91).
[17]Origen, *Homilies on Genesis* 3.2 (91).
[18]Origen, *Homilies on Joshua*, ed. Cynthia White, trans. Barbara J. Bruce, FC 105 (Washington, DC: Catholic University of America Press, 2002), 23.1 (195).
[19]Origen, *Homilies on Joshua* 23.1 (196).

received their portions by way of casting lots. And Origen adds the theologically weighty comment that "that lot (*sors*) is not tossed by chance, but according to that which was predestined (*prædestinatum*) by God."[20] Origen then goes through several additional biblical occurrences of casting lots: Jonah was selected by lot to be cast into the sea; Solomon appeals to the lot in the book of Proverbs (Prov 18:18); and the apostles filled the place of Judas by casting the lot. Origen concludes that "when prayer preceded, it was no longer by chance (*casu*) but by providence (*providentia*) that the lot announced divine judgment."[21]

Origen links this providential ordering of the lot to Christology: "But still I sought in the New Testament if anywhere the lot is mentioned in relation to Christ or to the Church, or even to mystic things that seem to relate to the soul."[22] He notes that several passages speak of our predestination "by lot" (*sorte*).[23] Origen insists that we should take these New Testament texts not just in their historical sense: "According to the inner understanding (*interiorem . . . intellectum*), as Paul seems to indicate when he says, 'in the portion of the lot of the saints' [Col 1:12], and 'called by lot in Christ' [Eph 1:11], it must be seen whether perchance the lot is drawn not only among humans, but also among the celestial powers."[24] Apparently, the drawing of lots here on earth reflects lots drawn in heaven. This explains how Deuteronomy 32:8 can say that God divided the nations and fixed the boundaries of the nations "according to the number of the angels of God." "We must not think," insists Origen, "that it was by accident (*per sortem*) that it indeed fell to one angel to receive by lot one nation, for example, that of the Egyptians, but to another, the nation of the

---

[20]Origen, *Homilies on Joshua* 23.1 (196).

[21]Origen, *Homilies on Joshua* 23.2 (197).

[22]Origen, *Homilies on Joshua* 23.2 (197).

[23]Origen, *Homilies on Joshua* 23.2 (197). Eph 1:11 uses the verb klēroō (to cast a lot); Col 1:12 speaks of a "share in the allotment" (klēros).

[24]Origen, *Homilies on Joshua* 23.3 (198); brackets added.

Idumeans, and to another, the nation of the Moabites and to another, India or every single nation on earth."[25] Origen draws from this a significant conclusion about divine providence, namely, "that not even for a single one of us does anything come to pass except by a lot of this kind that is dispensed by the judgment of God."[26] Therefore, when by lot Benjamin receives Jerusalem and Mount Zion (Josh 18:28), this is not just an accidental matter: "Doubtless, it is because the nature of that heavenly Jerusalem established it that the earthly Jerusalem, which preserved a figure and form of the heavenly one, ought to be given to none other than Benjamin."[27] (Origen has in mind Heb 10:1; 12:22, which he has just quoted.) Divine providence arranges human affairs by heavenly lots, so that earthly arrangements reflect heavenly arrangements. Within this divine economy, earthly lots function as types that resemble heavenly archetypes.

In *Homily* 25, Origen turns to Joshua 21, where by lot the Levites are assigned forty-eight cities in the Promised Land. Origen is at pains to point out that this casting of lots is in no way arbitrary or accidental. Among the sons of Levi—Kohath, Gershon, and Merari—Aaron and his sons, the priests, receive the first lot. Then follow the rest of the Kohathites, after which come the Gershonites, followed by the Merarites. Origen observes that a similar ranking had been in place in the wilderness when the Levites were distributed in ranked positions around the ark.[28] Origen comments: "You see how much order and how much consequence is maintained of things in Holy Scripture, how nothing is done except by measure and with reason and order."[29] Kohath, then, rightly obtains the first lot: "Whose lot was it suitable to be the first to fall out? To whom was it fitting to be given first place, if not to Aaron, the first high priest, first in life, in merits, first in

[25]Origen, *Homilies on Joshua* 23.3 (198-99).
[26]Origen, *Homilies on Joshua* 23.3 (199).
[27]Origen, *Homilies on Joshua* 23.4 (200).
[28]Origen refers to Num 3:38; 10:1-8. *Homilies on Joshua* 25.1 (209-10).
[29]Origen, *Homilies on Joshua* 25.1 (210).

honors and power? Is it resolved among you now at least that this casting of lots is not accidental (*fortuita*) but that a heavenly power is present, governing it according to the judgment of divine providence (*providentiæ judicium*)?"[30] For Origen, the casting of lots for Levitical cities has nothing accidental but takes place in accordance with divine providence. After explaining in exhaustive detail which tribes offer cities to which sons of Levi, Origen exclaims: "Who is able to follow and to comprehend all these things? Who can even remember and pay attention to the order of the mysteries (*mysteriorum*)?"[31] My hunch is that these words may well have echoed the wearied sentiment of his hearers.

Still, the providential division by lots is important to Origen precisely because they are mysteries or sacraments. Because earthly lots mirror an eternal providential ordering, they mirror also the future inheritance of the saints: "What do we say concerning those sacraments (*sacramentis*) that are depicted through this, and in which the distributions of a future inheritance are dimly sketched, and through which the division of the holy land that 'the meek' receive 'by inheritance' will be made known?"[32] Providence is God's loving guidance of his people to eternal life. "The prime significance of providence for Origen," insists John McGuckin, "lies in its pedagogical value and its soteriological end."[33] How does lot casting prefigure the aim of the resurrection? Also in the resurrection, Origen claims, nothing will be done "haphazardly" (*confuse*); also there, everyone will come "in his own order" (see 1 Cor 15:23),[34] and the ranking will be similar to the way in which the tribes and Levites had been placed in order of importance around the ark in the wilderness.[35]

---

[30]Origen, *Homilies on Joshua* 25.2 (210).

[31]Origen, *Homilies on Joshua* 25.4 (212-13).

[32]Origen, *Homilies on Joshua* 25.4 (213).

[33]Stamenka Antonova, "Providence," in *The Westminster Handbook to Origen*, ed. John Anthony McGuckin (Louisville, KY: Westminster John Knox, 2004), 182.

[34]Origen, *Homilies on Joshua* 25.4 (213).

[35]Origen, *Homilies on Joshua* 25.4 (213).

For Origen, then, the casting of lots and the manner in which the tribes are hierarchically ordered mirrors both divine providence and the life of the resurrection. This is hardly surprising. In Christian Platonic fashion, Origen's cosmology functions by way of an *exitus-reditus* schema. The biblical narrative serves, on this understanding, as the sacramental means that links the point of origin with the point of return. The eternal Logos is for Origen the source of an economy of salvation that unfolds in a display of divine care and provision, while in the eschaton everything folds back into the life of God in Christ—healed, renewed, and matured by the providential journey of salvation. For Origen, the biblical narrative (and, indeed, the very words of Scripture) serves as sacramental provision that already makes present the life of God who is both source and end.

SCRIPTURE AMONG OTHER BOOKS

Origen's theology of Scripture as providential sacrament has implications for how we read Scripture. As we have seen, the purpose of biblical words is to make present the Word of God, God's eternal providence, and so to lead us back to God. Therefore, it is important for Bible readers to be in sync with the divine Logos as they enter the biblical text.[36] The Word becomes present in our souls when our lives are in harmony with the providential Word of God in Scripture. Michael Graves puts it this way:

> Scripture is applied to "the mediating activity of the *Logos*," which both reveals the *logos* to the individual (so that it is self-revealing) and leads the soul through progressive stages to moral and mystical perfection (cf. Origen's Platonism). The task of exegesis for Origen is to allow the hearers of Scripture to receive this instruction from the *logos*. Thus, Origen's expositions often follow a basic trajectory moving from the literal

---

[36]See Karen Jo Torjesen, *Hermeneutical Procedure and Theological Method in Origen's Exegesis*, PTS 28 (Berlin: de Gruyter, 1986), 130-34.

sense, as defined by the nature of the book being studied, to the spiritual sense, which is presented in such a way as to lead the soul to progress toward perfection.[37]

Origen's common allegorical move from history to spirit is the direct result of his conviction that Scripture participates in divine providence, so that the eternal Word of God makes himself uniquely present here.

True, Origen's hermeneutic builds on Philo's allegorical approach and on a Stoic understanding of providence. The reason, however, that Origen found them useful is that he was convinced that they helped him interpret Scripture in the light of Christ as the incarnation of the Word and that they facilitated the reader's journey toward the eschatological telos of perfection. The providential sacramentalism undergirding Origen's exegesis, therefore, is primarily a *theological* principle leading to a *theological* mode of interpretation that is centered on Christ. Christ, after all, is the incarnation of the Logos *par excellence*. The incarnation transforms the surface of the biblical text so that its deeper, spiritual meaning becomes manifest. As Henri de Lubac puts it: "Just as one must not stop in Christ at the man who is seen but, through the flesh that veils him to carnal eyes, perceive by faith the God who is in him, so one must go through the external history that is offered to us in the Holy Books, particularly in the Old Testament, in order to penetrate to the 'spiritual mystery' that is hidden there."[38] This spiritual meaning was, for Origen, identical to the providential Logos, who, because he had manifested himself in the incarnation, could be found also in the text of Scripture. In the

---

[37]Michael Graves, "'Pagan' Background of Patristic Exegetical Methods," 104. The phrase in quotation marks comes from Torjesen, *Hermeneutical Procedure*, 118. Grove rightly suggests that Origen moves from the literal to the spiritual sense. It is also true that in some sense, the former is "defined by the nature of the book being studied." But for Origen the "nature of the book" is not explained by purely natural means but always already takes into account God's divine providence as we know it in Christ.

[38]De Lubac, *History and Spirit*, 105.

biblical text just as in the incarnate Christ, one could find the providential Logos, who is both the eternal origin and the final telos of divine providence.

At this point, the basic difference between patristic hermeneutics and much contemporary biblical exegesis should be evident. Contemporary historical exegesis for the most part does not reckon with divine providence. I don't mean that biblical scholars reject faith in providence; rather, providence doesn't in any way affect how they interpret the biblical text. Much contemporary biblical scholarship continues to treat exegesis merely as a search for authorial intent. While early Christian readers were not indifferent to human authorial intent, they placed it within the larger framework of divine intent. And God's intent or purpose for Scripture was understood to be providential: it was a means of grace meant to take the reader toward the incarnate Logos as revealed in Scripture and so to the spiritual purpose of the contemplation of God.

It is hardly surprising that exegesis has turned into a historical discipline. Providence has increasingly come to take a backseat in Western culture as a whole. I cannot sketch this development in detail here. Suffice it to say that heaven and earth have gradually drifted apart in the cultural mindset, beginning with late medieval nominalism, through the Reformation, and especially as a result of seventeenth- and eighteenth-century developments culminating in Deism and strict forms of naturalism. A robust notion of divine providence, one that maintains that the final end of creation is securely held in the mind of God, is increasingly cast aside. In the purely natural world that has emerged in modernity, it seems strange to read Scripture with a view to providential origin and end. John Webster is right, therefore, when he blames in part "the complex legacy of dualism and nominalism in Western Christian theology, through which the sensible and intelligible realms, history and eternity, were thrust away from each other, and creaturely forms (language, action, institutions) denied any capacity to indicate the presence and activity of the transcendent God."[39] Again, obviously many exegetes of the grammatical-historical school of interpretation continue to hold to divine providence as a doctrinal belief. However, they have largely lost the sense that this belief materially affects our mode of interpretation.

When in discussion with biblical colleagues I defend the notion that we need to search for Christ in all of Scripture (which is my polite way of saying it should be read allegorically), I repeatedly encounter the objection, "But you wouldn't treat any other text that way!" Whether consciously or not, the comment echoes Benjamin Jowett's well-known claim, made in 1860, that the interpreter's "object is to read Scripture like any other book."[40] Jowett, of course, was not the first to advocate a strictly nontheological reading of Scripture. Historicist exegesis had its first advocates in the seventeenth century, in Thomas Hobbes and Baruch Spinoza.[41] But Jowett's essay "On the Interpretation of Scripture" caused waves at least partly because of the direct and unequivocal manner in which he articulated his convictions:

> The office of the interpreter is not to add another [interpretation], but to recover the original one; the meaning, that is, of the words as they struck on the ears or flashed before the eyes of those who first heard and read them.... The history of Christendom is nothing to him; but only the scene at Galilee or Jerusalem, the handful of believers who gathered themselves together at Ephesus, or Corinth, or Rome. . . . All the after-thoughts of theology are nothing to him; they are not the true lights which light him in difficult places. . . . He has no theory

---

[39]John B. Webster, *Holy Scripture: A Dogmatic Sketch* (Cambridge: Cambridge University Press, 2003), 19-20.

[40]Benjamin Jowett, "On the Interpretation of Scripture," in *The Interpretation of Scripture and Other Essays* (New York: Dutton, 1907), 7.

[41]See Boersma, *Scripture as Real Presence*, 6-9. R. W. L. Moberly, too, points to Spinoza and others as predecessors to Jowett's maxim. "'Interpret the Bible Like Any Other Book?' Requiem for an Axiom," *JTI* 4 (2010): 92-93.

of interpretation; a few rules guarding against common errors are enough for him. His object is to read Scripture like any other book, with a real interest and not merely a conventional one. He wants to be able to open his eyes and see or imagine things as they truly are.[42]

On and on it goes. For Jowett, the aim was to take a time capsule to the era of the biblical author and to recover the original meaning that he had intended.

Jowett's insistence that we read the Bible like any other book is not entirely without warrant, as Walter Moberly points out. First, comments Moberly, "insofar as the axiom's purpose is to preclude special pleading of any kind, it plays a valuable role."[43] Presumably, we want to interpret the biblical text with integrity, without shortcuts, obfuscations, or anything of the sort. Second, Moberly acknowledges that we need to follow the standard rules of the grammatical syntax of the biblical languages.[44] And finally, he agrees that our interpretation should be in line with the literary genre that the biblical writers used.[45] All this seems right. What is more, even Jowett's concern with authorial intent is not without merit. Jowett wanted to know the original meaning of the text: "Educated persons are beginning to ask, not what Scripture may be made to mean, but what it does."[46] Jowett's unequivocal identification of meaning with original intent may be erroneous and naive, but he was right to suggest that authorial intent is an important element within a historical recovery of what the text meant.

Still, the phrase "educated persons" gives the game away. Divine providence gives Scripture not only to the educated but to the entire people of God. I will say more about the place of the church in the next chapter, but I should observe at this point that the Scriptures are

---

[42]Jowett, "On the Interpretation of Scripture," 6-7.
[43]Moberly, "'Interpret the Bible Like Any Other Book?'," 94.
[44]Moberly, "'Interpret the Bible Like Any Other Book?'," 94-95.
[45]Moberly, "'Interpret the Bible Like Any Other Book?'," 95.
[46]Jowett, "On the Interpretation of Scripture," 8.

not primarily a collection of historical documents whose original, historical meanings are to be teased out by a scholarly elite but a providential sacrament given to the people of God in canonical form, the meanings of which depend on its providential aim. Of course, these two are not each other's polar opposites and are not mutually exclusive: the Scriptures are both a collection of historical documents and a providential sacrament. The problem is not historical reading per se, but a historical reading that precludes divine providence as providing the primary setting and aim of biblical interpretation.

Reading the Bible "like any other book" typically assumes that general hermeneutics should override special or theological hermeneutics. But why that assumption? The starting point for biblical exegesis is not general but special hermeneutics. God's self-revelation in Christ is his final and definitive speech: "In these last days he has spoken to us by his Son" (Heb 1:2). Divine providence has taken flesh in Christ, and as a result it is this unique event in God's providential economy that forms the starting point for biblical exegesis. This doesn't mean that general hermeneutics has no bearing on biblical interpretation. As we have seen, Moberly rightly acknowledges that in some ways, we do read the Bible like any other book. But this observation comes *after* the recognition of God's providential economy in Christ. The supernatural end of providence precedes the shared natural and historical exigencies of everyday life.[47] For this reason, historical exegesis plays a legitimate, but subservient and secondary role in relation to the sacramental function that Scripture plays within the divine economy.

Reading the Bible like any other book—to the degree that this is a legitimate exercise—does not mean that the literal or the historical meaning is a strictly objective datum, waiting to be discovered through

---

[47]In Moberly's words, "The issue, in short, is the way in which when Christians think about and evaluate anything weighty and truth-claiming in life, then they (in principle) do so in the light of their understanding of God and humanity which is given in Jesus Christ" ("'Interpret the Bible Like Any Other Book?'," 101).

scientific means. The emphasis on "method" in biblical scholarship is often overdone. True, knowledge of ancient Near Eastern history, an eye for grammatical constructs, biblical-theological study of key themes of particular biblical books, and consultation of concordances and word studies are all helpful as we acquaint ourselves with a particular biblical passage. It is also true, I think, that historical investigation yields genuine insights (though they are always partial and approximate). But Hans-Georg Gadamer's *Truth and Method* (1960) has made clear that general hermeneutics involves a dialogic process, for which the methodology of the natural sciences does not offer an adequate paradigm.[48] In the humanities, and particularly when it comes to interpreting religious texts, the reader's own presuppositions invariably come into play, so that meaning occurs when the horizons of the text and those of the interpreter come together (*Horizontverschmelzung*).[49]

Andrew Louth, drawing on Gadamer for a spirited defense of allegorical exegesis, writes:

> The historical-critical method is, on the analogy of the scientific method, a way of reaching objective truth, that is, truth that inheres in the object, independently of the one who knows this truth. It is necessary, then, to locate the objectivity that it is the purpose of the method to reach. This is done by ascribing to the object of study, which in the humanities focuses on the writings of men, a "meaning" which is there independently of any understanding of it, an objective meaning which the historical-critical method attempts to discover.[50]

Louth's comments apply not only to historical criticism (which is very much on the wane anyway) but also to many other biblical

---

[48]Hans-Georg Gadamer, *Truth and Method*, 2nd ed., trans. Joel Weinsheimer and Donald G. Marshal (1975; repr., London: Continuum, 2011), 184-97, 231-42.

[49]See David Vessey, "Gadamer and the Fusions of Horizons," *IJPS* 17 (2009): 531-42.

[50]Andrew Louth, *Discerning the Mystery: An Essay on the Nature of Theology* (1983; repr., Oxford: Clarendon, 2003), 30.

scholars who regard it as their primary task to establish the original meaning of the text. Such scholarship too often takes on the mantle of a naturalist scientific methodology, and as such insufficiently appreciates that the results of historical exegesis are not just partial and approximate but also perspectival: the questions asked and the mode of investigation depend on the historian's own standpoint, and they shape the exegetical results.

Two sermons on the same text are rarely identical, even with regard to the historical exegesis that undergirds them. This is not a short-coming but a proper reflection of the infinitely varying personal horizons of the preachers. It is not just the move to the spiritual level, therefore, that leads to polyvalent meanings; polyvalence characterizes *literal* readings of Scripture as well. To be sure, in a postmodern context, polyvalence will often be tied to identity politics and relativism; but the proper response is not a lapse into modern historicism and objectivism. Instead, we may trust that from within the unique, particular location in which God places each one of us, we discern something of the divinely intended meaning of the text. Such an approach does not make human experience or context normative; we remain answerable to the divine Word that speaks to us. But by acknowledging our limited human horizons in interpretation, we recognize that historical investigation draws on the imagination as much as on analytical skill. Therefore, even when we come to Scripture with questions of history and authorial intent prominently in mind (and to that extent read it like any other book), we still should not expect a God's-eye view. Attempts to arrive at such a perspective are a practical denial of human finitude and subjectivity.

In the last several years, I have become interested in *lectio divina*, the spiritual reading practice as it flourished particularly within the medieval monastic tradition. *Lectio divina*, in the understanding of the twelfth-century Carthusian prior Guigo II, consists of four elements: reading (*lectio*), meditation (*meditatio*), prayer (*oratio*), and contemplation (*contemplatio*).[51] The meditative and prayerful reading that Guigo and others practiced was rather unlike the historical exegesis to which modernity has accustomed us. To be sure, Guigo was not opposed to careful study of the Bible. He describes the first stage, that of *lectio*, as follows: "Reading is the careful study of the Scriptures, concentrating all one's powers on it."[52] But Guigo's *lectio divina* does not "remain on the outside."[53] Instead, in *meditatio* it "goes to the heart of the matter," pondering the significance of the details of the text.[54] Next, in *oratio* one turns to the Lord and pleads with him, "When you break for me the bread of sacred Scripture, you have shown yourself to me in that breaking of bread, and the more I see you, the more I long to see you, no more from without, in the rind of the letter, but within, in the letter's hidden meaning."[55] Finally, in *contemplatio* the Lord graciously restores the soul, slaking its thirst and feeding its hunger, so that it becomes "wholly spiritual."[56]

It may be tempting to treat *lectio divina* as an esoteric kind of practice, a specialty for medieval monks and others with a particular interest in this type of reading. This way we would reserve for ourselves an understanding of exegesis as a scientific method of arriving at the historical meaning, while placing *lectio divina* into a special-interest box, entirely separate from exegesis. To Guigo (and other premodern readers), such compartmentalizing would have held no appeal. To be sure, one may observe in the twelfth and thirteenth centuries an increasing division between scholarship and piety, a gap that in modernity has become an unbridgeable gulf.[57] And without

---

[51]See Guigo II, *The Ladder of Monks: A Letter on the Contemplative Life and Twelve Meditations*, trans. and ed. James Walsh (Kalamazoo, MI: Cistercian Publications, 1982).

[52]Guigo II, *Ladder of Monks*, par. 2 (68).

[53]Guigo II, *Ladder of Monks*, par. 5 (70).

[54]Guigo II, *Ladder of Monks*, par. 5 (70).

[55]Guigo II, *Ladder of Monks*, par. 6 (72).

[56]Guigo II, *Ladder of Monks*, par. 7 (74).

[57]See Hans Urs von Balthasar, "Theology and Sanctity," in *The Word Made Flesh*, vol. 1 of *Explorations in Theology*, trans. A. V. Littledale with Alexander Dru (San Francisco: Ignatius, 1989), 181-209.

careful investigation of the biblical text in *lectio*, spiritual reading can lead to sentimentality. But the monks who practiced *lectio divina* rightly discerned that the Scriptures are meant to function as a sacramental means within God's broader providential economy. Rather than being an eccentric specialty for devotees, *lectio divina* tells all of us what Scripture is for and what we should do with it.

CONCLUSION

The Bible is both like and unlike any other book. I have already pointed to some of the similarities between the Bible and other books. One similarity I have not yet mentioned is that *all* books serve a providential role. If divine providence is as pervasive as Origen suggests—so that "God cares (*curare*) about mortal affairs and . . . nothing happens in heaven or earth apart from his providence (*providentia*)"[58]—then all human literary artifacts fall under God's care. This does not mean that all books are in line with the will of God; after all, as Origen also recognized, we can either align ourselves with God's good providence or refuse to accept his love—a moral maxim that holds true also for authors.[59] Still, in varying degrees the Word enters both writers and readers and allows books to participate in his providential care of the world. Since nature and the supernatural are inseparable, we must recognize that divine providence extends to other books as well as the Bible. In that sense, the Bible is like other books.

All books have a place within the providential economy. The French Dominican theologian Yves Congar points out that the patristic and medieval tradition had a keen awareness that the Holy Spirit is linked not just to Scripture but to a wide variety of writings. In an excursus on the term *inspiratio* in his book *Tradition and Traditions*, Congar explains that the terms *revelatio*, *inspiratio*, and *suggestio*

---

[58]Origen, *Homilies on Genesis* 3.2 (89).
[59]See Elliott, *Providence Perceived*, 22.

used to be applied in a much broader sense than they are in the modern period.[60] Terms such as *revelare, inspirare, illuminare,* and other analogous terms were "continually applied to the Fathers, councils, canons, even to the elections or particular acts of secular authorities."[61] These texts use the term *inspiratio* for canons and councils "because it applies to all those acts which represent a determination affecting the life of the Church."[62] Congar links this inspiration of the Spirit in the church as a whole with divine (providential) guidance: "The whole life of the Church is, in its successive stages of development, guided by the Holy Spirit."[63]

But Scripture is also unlike other books. The Scriptures are sacramental in a way that the Fathers, councils, and canons (let alone other writings) are not. From the beginning of the church, the Scriptures functioned in a unique manner, both within the liturgy and as a norm for doctrinal arbitration. Canonization may have been a slow process, but doctrinal disputes were always exegetical disputes about particular passages of the Old and New Testaments. Presumably, when Gregory of Nyssa refers to his brother Basil's *Hexaemeron* as "inspired" (*theopneuston*), or when the Council of Ephesus (431) describes its condemnation of Nestorius as "their inspired decision" (*autōn theopneustou kriseōs*), these statements were not meant to place patristic

---

[60]Yves M.-J. Congar, *Tradition and Traditions: The Biblical, Historical, and Theological Evidence for Catholic Teaching on Tradition* (San Diego, CA: Basilica, 1966), 119-37. See also Craig D. Allert, *A High View of Scripture? The Authority of the Bible and the Formation of the New Testament Canon* (Grand Rapids, MI: Baker Academic, 2007), 64-65.

[61]Congar, *Tradition and Traditions,* 119. Congar explains that terminology of revelation involved "the idea of divine illumination, active in all knowledge, even in what we should regard now as coming under the heading of purely natural knowledge." *Tradition and Traditions,* 122.

[62]Congar, *Tradition and Traditions,* 128.

[63]Congar, *Tradition and Traditions,* 129. Congar explains that the broader use of the term *inspiratio* continued into the Middle Ages and was still frequently found in the sixteenth century. *Tradition and Traditions,* 128. A change gradually set in through the Gregorian Reforms, initiating a "transition from this earlier appreciation of the ever active *presence of God* to that of *juridical powers* put at the free disposal of, and perhaps even handed over as its property to, 'the Church,' i.e. the hierarchy." *Tradition and Traditions,* 135.

writings and conciliar decisions on the same level as Scripture.[64] Yes, the same Spirit breathed in Basil and the Council of Ephesus as in the biblical authors. The words of Basil and Ephesus, too, participated in divine providence. But throughout the tradition of the church the biblical Scriptures have been recognized as uniquely inspired and hence been accorded unique authority.

It is because of its unique participatory role within divine providence —so that the Word of God shines through more clearly in Scripture than in any other human witness—that we read Scripture like we read no other book. Providence allows us to see the numerous different ways in which human speech functions in the divine economy and so helps us recognize that Scripture makes its own interpretive demands. Without providence, all we have is purely natural human writings, every one of them functioning on the same, flat surface of the natural world, none of them higher in hierarchical role than any others. Without providence, we have no words on which to stake our lives. Only when we confess God's supervening providential care and attention does it make sense to read Scripture with a view to the spiritual telos of divine authorial intent. No providence, no Scripture.

---

[64]Examples taken from Allert, *High View of Scripture?*, 64-65. Gregory goes on to say that Basil's work may surpass that of Moses in magnitude, beauty, complexity, and form, but this is likely rhetorical flourish. Throughout his writings, Gregory accords to Scripture a level of authority that he does not grant to his brother.

NO CHURCH, NO SCRIPTURE

DISTRUST OF TRADITION

Scripture is meant to be read in community. The universal church, spanning all ages and every culture, engages in the shared project of reading and interpreting the Bible. We cannot properly understand the Scriptures without the guidance of the catholic or universal church. This doesn't mean that we should never read Scripture on our own or should avoid scholarly issues in biblical interpretation. But it does mean that whether we read as individuals or in a communal setting, we are open to how the church more broadly has read the Bible. This ecclesial setting for biblical interpretation is crucial because apart from the church there is no Scripture and hence no valid interpretation: no church, no Scripture. *And so the fourth thing that I, as a theologian, wish biblical scholars knew is that the primary domain of reading Scripture is not the academy but the church.*

The argument of this chapter, then, is both anti-individualist (we read Scripture together as God's people) and anti-elitist (it is not scholars by themselves but the faithful together who derive meaning from Scripture). The two are invariably linked, and this chapter rejects both: the meaning that we derive as individuals from our reading of Scripture is neither primary nor determinative, and it is the church rather than the academy that provides the proper setting for biblical interpretation.

Distrust of tradition is in my genes. The strict, confessional Reformed tradition in which I grew up held unwaveringly to the *sola scriptura* maxim. I was convinced tradition invariably skews our understanding of the Bible. Only the careful, consistent use of the grammatical-historical method would yield the true meaning of the text. That I did relatively well in my studies gave me an extra confidence booster, convincing me that with consistent, patient use of the proper method I would be able not just to determine what the text really says but also to decide on the various doctrinal issues that have divided the church for centuries. Once in pastoral ministry, however, I began to realize that I perhaps had neither the time nor the ability to arrive at a well-thought-out position on the numerous issues on which I was supposed to have a biblical position. It took several humbling lessons before I began to realize that the adjudication of each and every exegetical and doctrinal issue was beyond my abilities.

In retrospect, my distrust of tradition stemmed from the equation of tradition with traditionalism. Convinced that Scripture comes from above and tradition from below, I opted for the former and wrote off the latter as human invention. (This doesn't mean that the creeds or the church's history were unimportant to me; but my *sola scriptura* position allowed me largely to repress the question of what kind of genuine authority they might have.) For Catholics to accept both Scripture and tradition as authoritative seemed to me to raise error-prone tradition to the level of infallible Scripture, thereby treating tradition as a source of divine revelation in addition to the Bible.

My Reformed view of Scripture versus tradition wasn't completely without warrant. Several biblical passages caution against adding to or taking away from Scripture (Deut 4:2; 12:32; Rev 22:18-19). Jesus chastises the Pharisaic custom of washing hands and utensils prior to eating as "tradition (*paradosis*) of the elders" (Mk 7:3, 5; see also Lk 11:37-53), which he equates with the "commandments of men" (Mk 7:7) to which Isaiah refers (Is 29:13).[1] And Saint Paul warns the Colossians not to be taken "captive by philosophy and empty deceit, according to human tradition (*paradosin tōn anthrōpōn*)" (Col 2:8). Some traditions deserve to be deconstructed.

In the case of Jesus' conflict with the Pharisees and lawyers, a combination of factors renders their tradition of washing hands and utensils problematic: they focus on externals rather than on the inside (Lk 11:40-41); they major in minors, neglecting the most significant teachings of the law (Lk 11:42); they love the public adulation that results from their tradition observance (Lk 11:43); they fail themselves to observe the traditions that they impose on others (Lk 11:46); and they introduce traditions as a way to circumvent the Decalogue (Mt 15:3-6; Mk 7:9-13). In short, Jesus assails the hypocrisy that is involved in his critics' traditions. His comments hardly constitute a wholesale rejection of tradition as such. After all, he explicitly insists that although tithing of mint, dill, and cumin may be a tradition that carries relatively little weight, the scribes and Pharisees are nonetheless right to observe it: "Woe to you, scribes and Pharisees, hypocrites! For you tithe mint and dill and cumin, and have neglected the weightier matters of the law: justice and mercy and faithfulness. These you ought to have done, without neglecting the others" (Mt 23:23).[2]

It is not easy to trace what precisely Saint Paul may have had in mind in warning against "human tradition" in Colossians 2:8. Whatever the historical backdrop, Paul's rejection of traditions in this passage associates it with "philosophy and empty deceit" and opposes

---

[1] Saint Paul uses the language of "the traditions of my fathers" in Gal 1:14.

[2] See the helpful discussion in Edith M. Humphrey, *Scripture and Tradition: What the Bible Really Says* (Grand Rapids, MI: Baker Academic, 2013), 31-34, 55-57.

it to Christ.[3] In line with the overall message of Colossians, it seems safe to suggest that Paul aims to uphold the all-sufficiency of Christ over against those who would add something to the God-given redeemer. Paul does not speak of "the traditions of men" here so as to play off Scripture against tradition. He has already positively used *tradition* language in Colossians 2:6, where he speaks of the Colossians having "received" (*parelabete*) Christ. The apostle wants the Colossians to uphold the tradition of Christ over against traditions that would undermine his sufficiency. Distrust of tradition is warranted when it supplements or undermines Christ as the center of the faith.

SCRIPTURE AND TRADITION

A strict *sola scriptura* position becomes difficult to maintain once we recognize that as a historical fact, Scripture lies embedded within the tradition.[4] In other words, in an important sense tradition precedes Scripture and as such has at least chronological priority over it. That is why in the second-century Polycarp's companion Papias inquired after the teaching of the Lord's direct disciples: "For I did not suppose that information from books helped me so much as that from a living and abiding voice."[5] Papias is referring to doctrines and morals passed on by the apostles. Prior to the canonization of the New Testament, the church was not without the contents of the gospel. It was passed on through the liturgy, through other practices and disciplines, and by means of episcopal succession.

---

[3]The current consensus seems to be that Saint Paul is reacting to Jewish ascetics (who may have been influenced by their pagan philosophical environment). See Peter T. O'Brien, *Colossians–Philemon*, WBC 44 (Waco, TX: Word, 1982), xxx-xli; James D. G. Dunn, *The Epistles to the Colossians and to Philemon: A Commentary on the Greek Text* (Grand Rapids, MI: Eerdmans, 1996), 23-35.

[4]Eugen J. Pentiuc uses the felicitous phrase "Scripture *(with)in* Tradition" and comments: "If Tradition is conceived as the life of the Holy Spirit in the Church, Scripture might be imagined as the Church's pulsating heart." *The Old Testament in Eastern Orthodox Tradition* (New York: Oxford University Press, 2014), 136.

[5]Eusebius of Caesarea, *Ecclesiastical History: Books 1–5*, trans. and ed. Roy Joseph Deferrari, FC 19 (Washington, DC: Catholic University of America Press, 1953), 3:39 (203).

The famous 1963 Montreal report on "Scripture, Tradition and Traditions" distinguishes between

> the Tradition (with a capital T), tradition (with a small t) and traditions. By the Tradition is meant the Gospel itself, transmitted from generation to generation in and by the Church, Christ himself present in the life of the Church. By tradition is meant the traditionary process. The term traditions is used in two senses, to indicate both the diversity of forms of expression and also what we call confessional traditions, for instance the Lutheran tradition or the Reformed tradition.[6]

With the first use of the term *Tradition* (capital *T*), we think of it as a noun: the contents of the gospel. The second understanding of *tradition* (small *t*) is more that of a verb: here we have in mind the process of traditioning or passing on. In a third sense, we speak of *traditions*, and here we focus on the adjective that precedes the term (e.g., Lutheran tradition or Reformed tradition).[7] Both as noun and as verb, T/tradition precedes the Scriptures historically.[8] Scripture has the role of presenting Tradition (Christ himself) and as such has a function within the tradition (the traditionary process).

It is impossible, therefore, to separate Scripture and T/tradition. Scripture contains Tradition (capital *T*). After all, Christ, or the gospel itself, is Scripture's contents. Scripture is also the most significant monument of the tradition (small *t*).[9] We cannot pull apart Scripture and T/tradition. Whether in terms of contents or transmission, they

---

[6]"Scripture, Tradition and Traditions," in *The Fourth World Conference on Faith and Order: The Report from Montreal 1963*, ed. P. C. Rodger and L. Vischer, Faith and Order Paper 42 (London: SCM Press, 1964), par. 39 (50).

[7]These associations of noun with contents, verb with activity of passing on, and adjective with particular confessional traditions were suggested to me by Rev. Doug Simmons.

[8]See "Scripture, Tradition and Traditions," par. 42 (51): "The very fact that Tradition precedes the Scriptures points to the significance of tradition, but also to the Bible as the treasure of the Word of God."

[9]See Yves Congar, *The Meaning of Tradition*, trans. A. N. Woodrow (1964; repr., San Francisco: Ignatius, 2004), 129-30.

are inseparable. My view of the relationship between Scripture and tradition, therefore, is one of coinherence.

Such a view rejects two alternatives. The one is what we might term the "supplementary view," which was prevalent in Catholicism from the time of the Council of Trent in the sixteenth century until the nineteenth century. On this understanding, God has revealed some teachings in Scripture, others in tradition. This view separates Scripture and tradition too neatly, as if there were two separate sources of divine revelation. It doesn't adequately do justice to Scripture's own status as one aspect of the tradition. It also runs the danger of introducing doctrines that have little or no grounding in Holy Scripture.

The other alternative is the "ancillary view" of Protestantism. Tony Lane describes this view by suggesting that the Reformers regarded "tradition not as a normative interpretation of Scripture nor as a necessary supplement to it but rather as a tool to be used to help the church to understand it."[10] This approach turns to tradition because it is a helpful source that can assist our own interpretation of Scripture. This is indeed an important function of tradition: we borrow from the wisdom of previous generations in our own interpretation of Scripture. Still, the term *ancillary* makes too tidy a split between Scripture and tradition. It ignores that Scripture is one of the monuments within the tradition and it isolates that one element in order to give it authoritative status all by itself. As a result, while it treats tradition as helpful in interpreting Scripture, it does not regard it as indispensable. (Far too often, biblical scholars today fail to make use of the tradition in their own exegesis altogether; helpful antidotes to such amnesia are the Ancient Christian Commentary Series, edited by Thomas C. Oden; *The Church's Bible*, edited by Robert L. Wilken; and the Reformation Commentary on Scripture, edited by Timothy George.)

---

[10]A. N. S. Lane, "Scripture, Tradition, and Church: An Historical Survey," *VE* 9 (1975): 43. I borrow the terms *supplementary* and *ancillary* view from Lane's article.

Small-*t* tradition, the church's act of transmitting the gospel message, carries on a redemptive movement that originates in the triune God. When on the day of his resurrection, Jesus comes through locked doors to appear to his disciples, he shows them his hands and his side and greets them: "Peace be with you. As the Father has sent me, even so I am sending you" (Jn 20:21). He then breathes on them, giving them the Spirit: "Receive the Holy Spirit. If you forgive the sins of any, they are forgiven them; if you withhold forgiveness from any, it is withheld" (Jn 20:22-23).[11] In this Johannine Pentecost, Jesus passes on the tradition: the Father sends the Son, who sends the apostles. Jesus' commissioning of the apostles is in line with his earlier high priestly prayer: "Sanctify them in the truth; your word is truth. As you sent me into the world, so I have sent them into the world" (Jn 17:17-18). The reliability of the subsequent tradition lies in Jesus' breathing—in his giving of the Spirit. Jesus does not leave the apostles as orphans (Jn 14:18). Their hearts need not be troubled (Jn 14:1, 27). When Jesus departs, he will leave them with the Helper (*paraklētos*), the gift of the Spirit, who will show them the gospel (Tradition): "The Helper, the Holy Spirit, whom the Father will send in my name, he will teach you all things and bring to your remembrance all that I have said to you" (Jn 14:26).

In the light of Jesus' giving of the Spirit, the overwhelmingly positive use of tradition language in Saint Paul is hardly surprising. In his second letter to the Thessalonians he encourages his readers, "Stand firm and hold to the traditions (*paradoseis*) that you were taught by us, either by our spoken word or by our letter" (2 Thess 2:15). Paul considered both his spoken words and his letters as means of passing on traditions. He commends the Corinthians for maintaining "the traditions" (*paradoseis*) precisely as he "delivered" (*paredōka*) them

---

[11]Edith Humphrey links the "reception" (*lambanō*) of the Spirit in Jn 20:22 to Jesus' "giving up" (*paradidōmi*) of the Spirit in Jn 19:30. *Scripture and Tradition*, 121. As we will see, in Saint Paul, *paradidōmi* and *paralambanō* function like a linguistic pair, denoting the passing on and reception of the gospel.

(1 Cor 11:2). Later in this same chapter, when he discusses the abuses surrounding the Lord's Supper in Corinth, the apostle introduces the words of institution by saying, "For I received (*parelabon*) from the Lord what I also delivered (*paredōka*) to you, that the Lord Jesus on the night when he was betrayed (*paredideto*) took bread" (1 Cor 11:23). Jesus was not just betrayed; he was traditioned or handed on. This traditioning of Jesus to death was both the cause and the contents of the Tradition (the gospel) that Paul received.

Saint Paul pairs the verbs *receive* (*paralambanō*) and *deliver* (*paradidōmi*) a second time, in 1 Corinthians 15: "For I delivered (*paredōka*) to you as of first importance what I also received (*parelabon*): that Christ died for our sins in accordance with the Scriptures, that he was buried, that he was raised on the third day in accordance with the Scriptures, and that he appeared to Cephas, then to the twelve" (1 Cor 15:3-5). Christ's death and resurrection were "in accordance with the Scriptures" and also were the actual Tradition that Paul has received and has passed on. The contents of capital-*T* Tradition are identical to that of the Scriptures. Both have at their core the paschal mystery. The gospel comes in twofold garb: both in writing and by means of oral tradition. Scripture and tradition cannot be separated.

We will get the Scripture-tradition relationship right only when we acknowledge that both are bound up with the church. After all, it is people (the church) that pass on the gospel (Tradition). Christian tradition is simply the dynamic process of the church continuing Christ's life through history. The coinherence that I've talked about so far is really a threefold coinherence, namely, of Scripture, tradition, and church. This raises the question of how exactly each of the legs of this three-legged stool (of Scripture, tradition, and church) functions in relation to the others. We've already seen that traditions can go awry. Similarly, church councils can and do err. (For an example, we only have to think of the so-called Blasphemy of Sirmium in the

year 357, when a council attempted to restore Arian teaching to ecclesial hegemony.) The Eastern church has it right, I think, when they
insist that only over time do councils attain authority. The church
needs to *receive* (*paralambanō*) council decisions, and this reception
process takes time.

This reception is a matter of discerning whether a decision is in
accordance with "the faith that was once for all delivered (*paradotheisē*)
to the saints" (Jude 3). Jesus' promise that the gates of hell shall not
prevail against the rock of church (Mt 16:18) implies a high view
of providence and trust in the church's tradition; but it does not entail
the belief that councils or popes never err. If that were the case, one
of the stool's legs would effectively trump the other two: the church's
magisterium would become the de facto source of all teaching. (This,
it seems to me, is the Catholic temptation.) A coinherence view insists
that this would lead to a wobbly stool, with one leg decidedly longer
than the other two. A coinherence view insists that church teaching
must always be grounded in Scripture and tradition.

Protestants typically run the opposite danger: they tend to saw off
not only the leg of tradition but also the leg of the church. *Sola
scriptura* all too often treats biblical interpretation as something that
as individuals we do on our own. But while it is certainly true that
individual people interpret Scripture, we are meant to do this within
the context of the church's tradition. One of the unique features of
the Bible is that it functions within the church with a particular
purpose. The Scriptures are God's means to equip the saints so as to
mature them spiritually and to lead them to eternal fellowship with
God. In other words, within the church the Scriptures have a sacramental function: they are a means of grace.

Saint Paul tells Timothy that the inspired Scriptures are "profitable
(*ōphelimos*) for teaching, for reproof, for correction, and for training
in righteousness, that the man of God may be complete, equipped for
every good work" (2 Tim 3:16-17). This text is usually discussed in

the context of inspiration. That's entirely legitimate, but we should keep in mind that Paul mentions inspiration as the backdrop to the Scriptures' profitability or usefulness. He underlines this by using five times the preposition *for* (*pros*) and by employing a purpose clause, which he introduces with the word *that* (*hina*; "that the man of God . . ."). Within the community of the church, we read the Scriptures with a particular purpose: teaching, reproof, correction, training—all with the ultimate aim of being equipped for good work.

The early church treated the usefulness (*ōpheleia*) of Scripture as one of the keys to interpretation. Biblical readers often insisted that one of the reasons to move from the letter to the spirit in one's exegesis is that often only the spiritual level gives us the text's usefulness. Mark Sheridan points out that the criterion of usefulness was prominent in Origen, Didymus the Blind, Gregory of Nyssa, Diodore, Theodore of Mopsuestia, Cyril, and Hesychius.[12] Sheridan gives the example from Origen's commentary on the story of Deborah in the book of Judges (Judg 4:4-6), where Origen quotes 2 Timothy 3:16 and then makes clear there is no "usefulness" in simply knowing the historical facts of Deborah being the "wife of Lappidoth," sitting "under the palm of Deborah between Ramah and Bethel in the hill country of Ephraim."[13] He therefore proceeds with an allegorical reading of these details.[14]

In the prologue to his sermons on the Song of Songs, Gregory of Nyssa too homes in on the notion of usefulness. He acknowledges: "If there is profit (*ōpheloiē*) even in the text taken for just what it says, we

---

[12]Mark Sheridan, *Language for God in Patristic Tradition: Wrestling with Biblical Anthropomorphism* (Downers Grove, IL: IVP Academic, 2015), 227.

[13]Origen, *Homilies on Judges*, ed. Thomas P. Halton, trans. Elizabeth Ann Dively Lauro, FC 119 (Washington, DC: Catholic University of America Press, 2010), 5.1 (76). See also Sheridan, *Language for God*, 228.

[14]Origen explains that Deborah's name (meaning "bee" or "speech") refers to the sweet honeycombs of prophetic teaching. Prophecy has a seat under the palm tree because the psalmist compares the righteous to a palm tree (Ps 92:12). This prophecy has its place between the "heights" (Ramah) and the "house of God" (Bethel). *Homilies on Judges* 5.2-3 (77-78).

have what is sought right before us."[15] The plain meaning, however, is not always "profitable" (*eis ōpheleian*), since Scripture often presents matters "by way of enigmas and below-the-surface meanings."[16] When Gregory discusses the Song's statement, "As an apple tree among the trees of the forest, so is my beloved among the young men" (Song 2:3), he rhetorically questions what this text could possibly be driving at: "What guidance in virtue would there be in this, unless there were some idea profitable (*ōphelountōn*) for us contained in the words?"[17] Hubertus Drobner rightly suggests that for Gregory of Nyssa, the first principle of allegorical exegesis had to do with usefulness. "At the beginning," writes Drobner, "the question of utility (ὠφέλεια) is asked."[18]

Modern historical readings typically assume that it is the individual, and perhaps only the individual scholar, who determines the true meaning of the biblical text. The *usefulness* of the text, on this understanding, is to find out what it meant historically. Within the communal body of the church, however, the *usefulness* of the text is not something buried in the past but something aimed at in the future: for the church fathers, the purpose, the usefulness, was to equip the saints for every good work. To be sure, whenever historical insights contribute to the greater spiritual usefulness, they too have their own (limited) usefulness. But it is the communal aim of entering into the divine life that determines what the text is for. Scripture's communal or ecclesial role is sacramental in character—it aims at the reality of the beatific vision. It simply won't do to substitute as the task of exegesis individual aims for this communal purpose.

---

[15]Gregory of Nyssa, *Homilies on the Song of Songs*, trans. and ed. Richard A. Norris, Writings from the Greco-Roman World 13 (Atlanta: Society of Biblical Literature, 2012), preface 4 (3).

[16]Gregory of Nyssa, *Homilies on the Song of Songs* preface 5 (3).

[17]Gregory of Nyssa, *Homilies on the Song of Songs* 4.125 (139).

[18]Hubertus R. Drobner, "Allegory," in *The Brill Dictionary of Gregory of Nyssa*, ed. Lucas Francisco Mateo-Seco and Giulio Maspero, trans. Seth Cherney, VCSup 99 (Leiden: Brill, 2010), 24. See also my more extended discussion in *Embodiment and Virtue in Gregory of Nyssa: An Anagogical Approach* (Oxford: Oxford University Press, 2013), 66-70.

CANONICAL READING

The communal or ecclesial context of reading Scripture comes to the fore in a variety of ways. Here I want to point out just three key elements: canon, liturgy, and creeds. First, the ecclesial context becomes clear in a canonical approach to exegesis. Canonical exegesis is often associated with the post-liberal or Yale school of interpretation, and in particular with scholars such as Hans Frei, George Lindbeck, Brevard Childs, and, more recently, Christopher Seitz. Frei's book *The Eclipse of Biblical Narrative* (1974) documents the eighteenth- and nineteenth-century shift in historical consciousness and its implications for the reading of Scripture.[19] Whereas once the literal sense of Scripture had been taken as a realist narrative that was centered on Christ, modernity forced biblical scholars to look at the history behind the narrative, which raised questions about the historical accuracy of the biblical account. As a result, liberal interpretation of Scripture became interested in uncovering universal moral lessons more than in the meaning of the narrative itself: "From now on, the harmony of historical fact, literal sense, and religious truth will at best have to be demonstrated; at worst, some explanation of the religious truth of the fact-like description will have to be given in the face of a negative verdict of its factual accuracy or veracity."[20] The increasing focus on the history behind the text meant that historical fact, literal sense, and religious truth could no longer present one unified picture.

Frei's historical account received philosophical and theological support from George Lindbeck. He focused on interpretation as a communal, linguistic event and as a result highlighted the centrality of the church as the context for interpreting Scripture. The result was what we may call a "pragmatic" view of what counts as proper interpretation: "What builds up the Church is what counts," argued

---

[19]Hans W. Frei, *The Eclipse of Biblical Narrative: A Study in Eighteenth and Nineteenth Century Hermeneutics* (New Haven, CT: Yale University Press, 1974).

[20]Frei, *Eclipse of Biblical Narrative*, 56.

Lindbeck, echoing the patristic focus on *ōpheleia*.[21] This is not to say that in all things the Yale school is in line with the early church. The church fathers, as a result of their Platonic proclivities, were much more uncompromising than post-liberals about the doctrine that the Bible teaches. Lindbeck's cultural-linguistic approach treats doctrine as mere grammar rules regulating the God-talk of particular communities. For Christian Platonists, by contrast, the church's truth claims participate in eternal truth and so are more than shared cultural-linguistic rules. Nonetheless, considering the near-undisputed reign of historical criticism in the nineteenth century, post-liberalism's focus on the ecclesial context of interpretation is a welcome antidote to the scholarly individualism that has dominated biblical studies far too long.

The Old Testament theologian Brevard Childs, also from Yale, arrived at the conclusion that historical investigation alone cannot give us the full meaning of the text, and that we should, therefore, take another look at pre-critical exegesis. For Childs, patristic exegesis (including allegory) had its own, inherent significance and could not be written off as an outmoded steppingstone leading toward contemporary historical-critical interpretation. His so-called canonical approach—set forth in books such as *Introduction to the Old Testament as Scripture* (1979) and exegetically exemplified in *The Book of Exodus* (1974) and *Isaiah* (2001)—is another influential example of the church's communal acknowledgment of the status of the biblical books guiding our interpretation.[22]

Christopher Seitz builds on Childs's work when he observes three facets in the canonical approach. The first aspect is literary-exegetical. Childs emphasized that canonical reading does not mean to deny or ignore the value of historical-critical interpretation. While agreeing with his teacher, Seitz nonetheless maintains that, unlike

---

[21]As quoted in David Lauber, "Yale School," in *DTIB*, 860.

[22]See Brevard S. Childs, *Introduction to the Old Testament as Scripture* (Philadelphia: Fortress, 1979); *The Book of Exodus: A Critical, Theological Commentary* (Philadelphia: Westminster, 1979); *Isaiah: A Commentary* (Louisville, KY: Westminster John Knox, 2001).

historical-critical approaches, "canonical reading does not seek authorial intent at the level of the text's prehistory."[23] Canonical reading,
Seitz maintains, "reckons that the final form [of the canon] is itself
a statement, fully competent to judge and constrain the prehistory
reconstructed by such [historical] methods."[24] The second facet is
catholic-ecclesial. Here, Seitz emphasizes that canonical interpretation is keen to learn from precritical readers. Reading always has a
social component, which means that there are social standards for
reading; the tradition has referred to this as the "rule of faith." This
means, for Seitz, that "canonical reading may find itself open to allegorical and figural interpretations, such as emerged in an earlier
day."[25] The last facet is theological. Seitz insists that we need to take
seriously the theological goal and underpinnings of exegesis, which
means we dare not ignore "the final arrangement and presentation
of the individual writings and collections in the canon."[26]

Childs and Seitz are correct: the canonical arrangement of the
biblical books is not an indifferent matter. The main reason that we
are reading (and interpreting) these particular books rather than
others is that the church has accepted these books as regulative for
its faith and life. Wherever historical criticism dominates, the question
invariably arises: But why are you reading this text? A purely scholarly,
historical mode of exegesis fails to take account of the Scriptures'
canonical composition. Ecclesial exegesis will recognize this canonical shape as providentially guided and will not hesitate to draw
concrete consequences from it.

We see an example of treating the Bible as a divinely intended unit
in the way that church fathers would scour the Scriptures in search
of words and passages that might shed greater light on a given biblical
text. In their book *Sanctified Vision*, John O'Keefe and R. R. Reno

---

[23]Christopher Seitz, "Canonical Approach," in *DTIB*, 100.
[24]Seitz, "Canonical Approach," 101.
[25]Seitz, "Canonical Approach," 101.
[26]Seitz, "Canonical Approach," 102.

refer to this as "associative reading."[27] Saint Augustine employs it throughout his writings. Robert Wilken mentions Augustine's use of the term "cleave" (*adhaerere*) in the Vulgate of Psalm 73:28—"For me to *cleave* to God is good."[28] The word reminds the bishop of Hippo of the end-time promise of Jeremiah: "I will be their God, and they shall be my people" (Jer 31:33; cf. Lev 26:12), and he insists that this promise is the reward that the psalm too has in view. The reason? "There can be no better good, no happier happiness than this: life for God, life from God, who is the well of life, in whose light we shall see light [Ps 36:9]."[29] For Augustine, because the promise of cleaving to God is fulfilled in eternal happiness (the beatific vision), it is legitimate to link Psalm 73:8 with Jeremiah 31 and with Psalm 36.

Nor is this all. Because eternal happiness is life in God, Augustine immediately moves into a trinitarian meditation: "Of that life the Lord himself says, 'This is life eternal, that they may know thee the one true God, and Jesus Christ whom thou hast sent' [Jn 17:3]."[30] This passage of John 17 sends Augustine in turn to John 14:21: "That is his own promise to his lovers: 'He that loveth me, keepeth my commandments; and he that loveth me is loved of my Father, and I will love him and will show myself unto him'—show himself in the form of God whereby he is equal to the Father, not in the form of a servant whereby he showed himself to the ungodly also."[31] The saints' eternal vision of Christ results from their love of Christ. By cleaving or adhering to the commandments, the believers join the mutual cleaving of Father and Son.[32] This joining of the trinitarian life is the result of

[27]John J. O'Keefe and R. R. Reno, *Sanctified Vision: An Introduction to Early Christian Interpretation of the Bible* (Baltimore, MD: Johns Hopkins University Press, 2005), 66.

[28]Robert Louis Wilken, *The Spirit of Early Christian Thought: Seeking the Face of God* (New Haven, CT: Yale University Press, 2003), 72-74.

[29]Augustine, *The Letter and the Spirit*, in *Augustine: Later Works*, trans. and ed. John Burnaby, LCC 8 (Philadelphia: Westminster John Knox, 1955), 22.37 (222); brackets added.

[30]Augustine, *Letter and the Spirit* 22.37 (222); brackets added.

[31]Augustine, *Letter and the Spirit* 22.37 (222).

[32]Augustine does not use the language of "cleaving" (*adhaerere*) to speak of the believers "keeping" the commandments or of the coinherence between Father and Son. It seems likely, however, that the term *adhaerere* triggers these intertextual references in Augustine's mind.

God giving man the gift of the Spirit, comments Augustine with reference to Romans 5:5, so that "he may be fired in heart to cleave (*inhaerere*) to his Creator, kindled in mind to come within the shining of the true light."[33]

Saint Augustine detects this same cleaving in 1 Corinthians 6:17, where the apostle warns against "cleaving" (*adhaerere*) to a prostitute. Speaking on this text in *Sermon* 162, Augustine again turns to Psalm 73, since Asaph too mentions fornication, not in a bodily sense but in the broader sense of unfaithfulness to God:[34]

> General fornication, then, is plainly indicated in the psalm, where it says, *Since behold, those who set themselves far from you shall perish; you have destroyed everyone who fornicates* (fornicatur*) away from you*; and where he goes on to show in what way this general fornication can be avoided and shunned, by adding, *But for me it is good to cleave* (adhaerere*) to God* (Ps 73:27-28). From this we can easily remark that what general fornication means for the human soul is for anyone not to cleave to God, but to cleave to the world.[35]

Augustine's contrast between cleaving to God and cleaving to the world is based on his association of 1 Corinthians 6 with Psalm 73: he detects a twofold verbal similarity (*fornicare* and *adhaerere*) as well as obvious theological similarities between Paul's letter and the psalm. In all, it should be clear that Augustine's playful weaving together of a variety of biblical texts makes sense only within a hermeneutical stance that highlights the canonical unity of the Bible.

Such associative reading was by no means limited to the North African bishop. It was ubiquitous among the church fathers. Elsewhere I have noted examples from Origen, Athanasius, Gregory of

---

[33]Augustine, *Letter and the Spirit* 3.5 (197).

[34]Psalm 73:27 uses the verb *zanah*, which means "to commit fornication, be a harlot" (BDB).

[35]Augustine, *Sermon* 162.3, in *Sermons*, ed. John E. Rotelle, trans. Edmund Hill, WSA III/5 (Hyde Park, NY: New City Press, 1992), 148.

Nyssa, and Cyril of Alexandria.[36] These could easily be multiplied by others. Gregory the Great continued the practice in the sixth century, and via Gregory this associative reading shaped medieval exegesis.[37] Recognizing that Christ is the reality to which the Old Testament points, premodern readers would typically interpret a word from the Old Testament Scripture by looking in the New Testament for similar or identical terms, recognizing that these terms might well shed light on the deeper meaning of the Old Testament text. Allegorical interpretation, therefore, was generally not arbitrary in character. Instead, it was based on the theological recognition of the unity of the church's canon, which provided justification for associative reading.

Verbal association did not function in isolation (and when it did, allegorizing tended to go off the rail). Usually the church fathers observed alongside verbal association a theological (often christological) connection. The reason they thought a particular verbal similarity sheds light on the biblical text is that the christological reality (*res*) illumines the Old Testament sacrament (*sacramentum*). Jean Daniélou, therefore, distinguishes between "illustrative" and "theological" typology. He explains that the mere mention of water somewhere in the Old Testament would not have been enough for the church fathers to detect a reference to baptism. Typology functions properly, according to Daniélou, when a theological similarity accompanies the illustrative (or verbal) similarity.[38] On my reading of the church fathers, the theological similarity for which they searched was primarily a christological one. These patristic insights are hardly a historical

---

[36]Hans Boersma, *Scripture as Real Presence: Sacramental Exegesis in the Early Church* (Grand Rapids, MI: Baker Academic, 2017), 180-82, 241-47, 253-54.

[37]Robert Louis Wilken goes so far as to suggest, "The technique Gregory uses most often for 'finding' or 'inventing' as he expounds the text is word association." "Interpreting Job Allegorically: The *Moralia* of Gregory the Great," *ProEccl* 10 (2001): 220. Wilken provides several examples from Gregory's *Moralia in Job*.

[38]Jean Daniélou, *The Bible and the Liturgy* (Notre Dame, IN: University of Notre Dame Press, 1956), 71-72, 78-79. I do not accept Daniélou's now-discredited distinction between allegory and typology.

curiosity; they have abiding value. It is the combined recognition of the Scriptures as a providentially determined canonical whole and of Christ as the sacramental reality of the Old Testament shadows that provides the justification for the practice of verbal association.

LITURGY AND CREEDS

A second example of the significance of the communal or ecclesial context for exegesis is the role of the liturgy. It is commonly recognized that "liturgical use" is one of the criteria that determined whether or not a particular book ended up in the New Testament canon. Lee Martin McDonald goes so far as to suggest, "The widespread use of the New Testament writings in the churches may have been the most determinative factor in the canonical process."[39] From the beginning, the Scriptures had their primary function within the life and liturgy of the church. The very structure of the liturgy was determined by Scripture, with the first half designed as "Liturgy of the Word" and the second half as "Liturgy of the Eucharist." So tight was the link between Scripture and liturgy from the outset that apart from liturgical use there would be no Scripture. Scripture is intended for use in the liturgy.

Too often, biblical exegesis, particularly of the Protestant grammatical-historical kind, operates on the assumption that (scholarly) exegesis directly leads to doctrine. Not infrequently, the role of the liturgy is overlooked as an aspect of the process through which Scripture yields doctrine. The ancient maxim of *lex orandi, lex credendi*—"the rule of prayer is the rule of faith"—suggests that this process is complex. The rule of faith (that which we believe) derives not from Scripture in isolation but from Scripture as it functions within the liturgy and the life of the church. Prosper of Aquitaine,

---

[39]Lee Martin McDonald, "Identifying Scripture and Canon in the Early Church: The Criteria Question," in *The Canon Debate*, ed. Lee Martin McDonald and James A. Sanders (Peabody, MA: Hendrickson, 2002), 432. The other three commonly recognized criteria are apostolicity, orthodoxy, and antiquity.

the fifth-century follower of Augustine who stands behind the well-known Latin aphorism, treated the liturgy as something to protect and safeguard because it conveys not just outward rites but also theological truths: "Let us look at the sacred testimony of priestly intercessions which have been transmitted from the apostles and which are uniformly celebrated throughout the world and in every catholic church; so that the law of prayer (*lex . . . supplicandi*) may establish a law for belief (*legem credendi*)."[40] The maxim *lex orandi, lex credendi* intimates that doctrine is not a free-floating, abstract theory but is grounded within the concrete particularity of the church's liturgical life.

Prosper of Aquitaine may be the historical source behind the *lex orandi, lex credendi* motto, but he was hardly the only church father to appeal to the liturgy in defense of Christian doctrine. Geoffrey Wainwright points out that such appeals were common in the early church. He first mentions Augustine and Ambrose as often referring to the teaching power of the liturgy. Wainwright next alludes to the mystagogical catechesis of Cyril of Jerusalem, Ambrose of Milan, John Chrysostom, and Theodore of Mopsuestia. And Wainwright refers in addition to Basil the Great, Optatus of Milevis, Tertullian, Irenaeus, and Ignatius of Antioch.[41] One example, from Jerome's *Dialogus contra Luciferianos*, may suffice by way of illustration. Jerome asks rhetorically:

> Are you unaware that it is a custom of the churches that hands should afterwards be laid on the baptized and the Holy Spirit be thus invoked? Do you ask where it is written? In the Acts of the Apostles. Even if no scriptural authority existed for it, the agreement of the whole world in the matter would have

---

[40]Prosper of Aquitaine, *De gratia Dei et libero voluntatis arbitrio* 11 (PL 51.209C), quoted in Geoffrey Wainwright, *Doxology: The Praise of God in Worship, Doctrine, and Life* (New York: Oxford University Press, 1980), 225.

[41]Wainwright, *Doxology*, 224-35.

the value of precept. For many other things which are observed by tradition in the churches have acquired the authority of a scriptural law.[42]

For Jerome, the liturgical life of the church obviously carried significance in the upholding of Christian doctrine.

My aim is not a straightforward defense of Jerome's approach. In my view, the relationship between *lex orandi* and *lex credendi* is a two-way street: doctrines always have a controlling function in developments in worship, because as we have already seen, traditions can and do go off the rails. Wainwright is surely right when he suggests that the magisterium "should actively promote liturgical forms which reflect the true faith, and it should nip in the bud any 'spontaneous' developments in worship which in its judgment distort the true faith."[43] Indeed, one of the ironies of the contemporary situation is that evangelicals, for whom traditionally the *lex credendi* holds priority, have largely abandoned its corrective function vis-à-vis liturgical worship. The latter is often treated as unrelated to doctrine and hence as infinitely malleable. In my view, the *lex credendi* affects the *lex orandi*.

Still, it is primarily the liturgy in which God makes himself present to us. As Alexander Schmemann points out, in the liturgy we ascend into heaven—not just symbolically, but truly. Schmemann points out that the altar is "the sign that in Christ we have been given access to heaven, that the Church is the 'passage' to heaven, the *entrance* into the heavenly sanctuary, and that only by 'entering,' by ascending to heaven does the Church fulfill herself, become what she is."[44] The liturgy is an ascent into heaven, into the eschaton. This means that in worship we truly join the angels and saints. Liturgy establishes created reality in a transfigured mode, the way it is meant to be, in the very

---

[42]Jerome, *Dialogus contra Luciferianos* 8 (PL 23.163C-164A), quoted in Wainwright, *Doxology*, 230.

[43]Wainwright, *Doxology*, 246-47.

[44]Alexander Schmemann, *For the Life of the World: Sacraments and Orthodoxy*, SVSPCS 1 (1973; repr., Yonkers, NY: St. Vladimir's Seminary Press, 2018), 41.

presence of God. If it is true that in the liturgy we enter most truly into the truth, goodness, and beauty of God, then Christian truth is most palpable in and through the liturgy, mostly in nonpropositional form. After all, sacramental reality (God in Christ), which becomes present to us in and through the Scriptures, becomes ours also in and through the eucharistic liturgy. This puts a great onus on us as we shape liturgical worship. And at the same time, it implies a calling to ensure that our beliefs conform to the church's liturgy.

Dennis Okholm, in his recent book *Learning Theology Through the Church's Worship*, deliberately shapes this introductory theology text with the help of the church's liturgy. His theological reasons for this approach are fourfold: (1) it reminds us to take a stance of humility; (2) it constantly places our theologizing under God's judgment; (3) it encourages a posture of listening to God; and (4) it makes us recognize our dependence on God's grace.[45] Each of these four elements makes the point that theology is merely the believer's grateful reception of God's revelatory gift of himself. Christian teaching is not the result of scholars mastering the biblical text. We arrive at genuine Christian teaching only when we have been in the presence of angels and saints and of the triune God himself. Only in the presence of divine light of the Spirit do the Scriptures begin to make sense to us.

The communal or ecclesial context for exegesis comes to the fore, third, in creedal guidelines for biblical interpretation. Baptism, in the early church, took place after the candidates had responded in the affirmative that they believed in the Father, the Son, and the Holy Spirit. Their faith in the triune God permitted them to be baptized "in the name of the Father and of the Son and of the Holy Spirit" (Mt 28:19). This same triadic structure shaped the "rule of faith" (*regula fidei*), which formed the basic outline for the early church's God-centered confession of faith. The various rules of faith—different

---

[45]Dennis Okholm, *Learning Theology Through the Church's Worship: An Introduction to Christian Belief* (Grand Rapids, MI: Baker Academic, 2018), 23-24.

forms of it occur in Irenaeus, Tertullian, Cyprian, and Novatian—all centered on the church's faith in the three persons of the one God. As Robert Jenson puts it: "The rule of faith, the *regula fidei*, was a sort of communal linguistic awareness of the faith delivered to the apostles, which sufficed the church for generations. This gift of the Spirit guided missionary proclamation, shaped instruction, identified heresy, and in general functioned wherever in the church's life a brief statement of the gospel's content was needed."[46] It is impossible to treat either the church's baptismal formula or its *regula fidei* simply as the outcome of a grammatical-historical interpretation of the biblical text.

From the outset, Scripture and creed were interconnected. Speaking of the slowly emerging New Testament canon in the early church, Jenson suggests: "The new canon and the rule of faith match like conversely notched puzzle pieces. Each advances what the other holds back. Canon and creed fitted together, and only canon and creed fitted together, could make and can now make one whole and integral guardian of the church's temporal self-identity."[47] Canon and creed, scriptural exegesis and ecclesial doctrine inform and enrich each other.

Over time, the rule of faith has been supplemented by the Nicene Creed, the Chalcedonian Formula, and the Apostles' Creed, as well as by the seven ecumenical councils and the broad patristic consensus. These authorities form ever-widening concentric circles that guide our interpretation of Scripture. I am not advocating subscription to particular confessional statements such as the Catechism of Trent, the Augsburg Confession, or the Westminster Standards. The reason is that although Catholic, Lutheran, and Reformed traditions each contribute unique insights to our understanding of Scripture, their distinctive characteristics are not universally agreed upon, which makes their authority limited in scope. Unlike the ecumenical

---

[46]Robert W. Jenson, *Canon and Creed* (Louisville, KY: Westminster John Knox, 2010), 15.
[47]Jenson, *Canon and Creed*, 41.

consensus of the early church, confessions from the Reformation period are not universally accepted and therefore are not binding for biblical interpretation today. Still, the theologians of the "confessional age" of the sixteenth and seventeenth centuries rightly saw that the church's faith ought to guide our exegesis and must provide parameters for it. We simply cannot defend Christian teaching without recourse to the creedal structures of the church. A strict *sola scriptura* position is erroneous not only because it invariably leads to a cacophony of interpretations, but also because it fails to take into account the particularities of the Spirit's faithful guidance of the church's historic pilgrimage to the eschaton.[48]

CONCLUSION

So, we witness the communal character of biblical exegesis in three ways: canon, liturgy, and creed. These together form the bedding that nourishes a proper reading of the Bible. The three have in common that each provides a powerful antidote to elitism. Perhaps the most fatal flaw of the application of scientific methodology to biblical exegesis is that it relies on an elite, academic guild to provide the one, correct meaning of the text. It would not be an overstatement to say that here the magisterium of the Roman Catholic Church has been replaced with the magisterium of the scientific guild.

Ironically, this elitism has its origin in the antielitist sentiments of Enlightenment philosophy. The Enlightenment was in part a reaction against the authority of the priesthood over the faithful. The Irish freethinking philosopher John Toland, in his 1696 book *Christianity Not Mysterious*, took aim at the clergy's claim to superior insight into the divine mysteries. Toland's book, therefore, was a broadside against

---

[48]See Jenson's comment: "That we treat dogma as almost creedal is a venture, undertaken by faith that the Spirit will not let the church err fatally or in the long term—but just so is indeed a risk, an aspect of the church's communal venture of faith. And if indeed we doubt or defend a dogma, our recourse must be to a *norma normans*, canon and creed together." *Canon and Creed*, 69.

clerical snobbery. As Toland saw it, one of the main reasons that Catholic clergy had recourse to mystery was the will to power. The clergy have labored hard, writes Toland, "not only to make the plainest, but the most trifling things in the World mysterious, that we might constantly depend upon them for the Explication."[49] As Toland saw it, starting with the second and third centuries, the clergy began to establish all manner of ceremonies and rites. They organized into a separate hierarchical body, pretending to be "Labourers in the Lord's Vineyard."[50] Feigning that the faithful needed them as intermediaries, "the Clergy were able to do any thing; they engross'd at length the sole Right of interpreting Scripture, and with it claim'd Infallibility, to their body."[51]

Toland's anticlericalism was the direct result of an unfettered appeal to human reason and was centered on the question of authority. His book was a biting attack on the authority of the magisterium. To make the Scriptures depend on the church for its authority, as the "Papists" did, obviously entailed a circular argument: "You must believe that the Scripture is Divine, because the Church has so determined it, and the *Church* has this deciding Authority from the Scripture. . . . Hey-day! are not these eternal Rounds very exquisite Inventions to giddy and entangle the Unthinking and the Weak?"[52] Toland's rationalism left no room for mystery and as a result couldn't conceive of circularity as coinherence.

Toland's rationalism exposed in the harshest of terms the clericalism of the medieval church. He failed to recognize, however, that at best he was replacing one form of elitism with another. From now on, the faithful would depend not on the church's clergy but on the academy's scholars. When we remove the ecclesial context of canon, liturgy, and creeds from hermeneutical consideration for the sake of recovering

---

[49]John Toland, *Christianity not Mysterious: Or, A Treatise Shewing, That there is nothing in the Gospel Contrary to Reason, Nor Above it: And that no Christian Doctrine can be properly call'd a Mystery* (London: Sam Buckley, 1696), 26.

[50]Toland, *Christianity not Mysterious*, 171; italics omitted.

[51]Toland, *Christianity not Mysterious*, 171; italics omitted.

[52]Toland, *Christianity not Mysterious*, 32; italics omitted.

the text's original meaning, the church invariably ends up at the mercy of a scholarly elite that determines the true meaning of the text.

Whatever the shortcomings of late medieval clericalism, the church cannot be at the mercy of the latest scholarly consensus (which is typically feeble and of short duration); intellectual elitism is foreign to the character of the church. David Steinmetz's famous words in the conclusion of his treatment of pre-critical exegesis are well worth repeating: "The medieval theory of levels of meaning in the biblical text, with all its undoubted defects, flourished because it is true, while the modern theory of a single meaning, with all its demonstrable virtues, is false. Until the historical-critical method becomes critical of its own theoretical foundations and develops a hermeneutical theory adequate to the nature of the text which it is interpreting, it will remain restricted—as it deserves to be—to the guild and the academy, where the question of truth can endlessly be deferred."[53] The church cannot afford to wait with the question of truth—and the good thing is this: the biblical text yields meaning not primarily as a result of scholarly insight (though this contributes) but through heavenly contemplation in the company of the saints.

I do not want to be misunderstood as disparaging historical or archeological study for the sake of deeper knowledge of the Scriptures. I simply want to suggest that a biblical interpreter is first and foremost not a historian but a theologian (who uses historical insights as one part of the interpretive process). The primary context for exegesis is not the academic guild but the church. Without the church, we would have nothing but antiquarian or sociological reasons to study *these* particular books and to refer to *them* as Scripture. It should be clear why I wish biblical scholars knew that the primary domain of reading Scripture is not the academy but the church: only in the church is the Bible the Bible. No church, no Scripture.

[53]David C. Steinmetz, "The Superiority of Pre-critical Exegesis," *Theology Today* 37 (1980): 38.

NO HEAVEN, NO SCRIPTURE

CONTEMPLATION AS *UNUM NECESSARIUM*

Action and contemplation together make up the Christian life. In this chapter, I will discuss the relationship between the two, and I will also ask the question of how biblical interpretation relates to both. I hope to make clear that although the active life (*vita activa*) and the contemplative life (*vita contemplativa*) feed into each other, the latter has a kind of priority: contemplation (love of God) is our final end. Contemplation, therefore, is the driving force that guides the active life (the life of virtue) and that guides also our reading of Scripture. The end of Bible reading lies penultimately in action and ultimately in contemplation. To be sure, as we will see, virtue plays a hugely significant role in the Christian tradition. Action and contemplation both center on the love of Christ, and both are indispensable, even if only the latter is our final end. The upshot of this understanding of action and contemplation is that biblical interpretation must always be guided by this love of Christ; the rule of charity (*regula caritatis*) is the primary factor determining our interpretation of Scripture. *The*

final thing that I, as a theologian, wish biblical scholars knew is that the
Bible cannot be read apart from its spiritual end, which is the heavenly
contemplation of God in Christ.

The above paragraph perhaps makes it look as though the active
life (*vita activa*) and the contemplative life (*vita contemplativa*) were
always in harmonious relationship. They should be, but in actual fact
they often are not. Scripture presents models for both: Martha and
Mary, Leah and Rachel, Peter and John—the first in each pair repre-
senting the active life, the second the contemplative life. Many of the
church's saints have struggled to keep the two in harmony. Saint Augustine was more or less forced into the active life of a bishop and
would have much preferred the life of a contemplative. The reason for
his preference is simple: Augustine associates *actio* with our present,
temporal life and *contemplatio* with future, eternal vision of God.[1] It's
no small wonder that Augustine would favor contemplation over
action. Still, he followed what he saw as God's call and committed
himself to the hustle and bustle of his episcopal task. With similar
reluctance, Saint Gregory the Great turned from monk to pope. He
often writes of his desire to devote more time to contemplation. In a
letter to Theoctista, the emperor's sister, he complains, "I have lost
the profound joys of my peace and quiet, and I seem to have risen
externally, while falling internally. Wherefore, I deplore my expulsion
far from the face of my Creator."[2] These struggles continue beyond
Augustine and Gregory into the Middle Ages and modernity. Invariably, the saints' desire is for more contemplation of God.

This longing indicates a priority of contemplation over action. After
all, "but one thing is necessary" (*unum necessarium*), and Mary has

---

[1] Kimberly F. Baker, "Augustine on Action, Contemplation, and Their Meeting Point in Christ"
(PhD diss., University of Notre Dame, 2007), 17.

[2] Gregory the Great, *Epistle* I.5, in *The Letters of Gregory the Great*, vol. 1, trans. and ed. John
R. C. Martyn, MST 40 (Toronto, ON: Pontifical Institute of Mediaeval Studies, 2004), 122.
See Gavin Ortlund, *Theological Retrieval for Evangelicals: Why We Need Our Past to Have a
Future* (Wheaton, IL: Crossway, 2019), 188-96.

chosen this "best part" (*optima pars* in the language of the Latin Vulgate; Lk 10:42). Mary's choice is in line with David's single-minded devotion to the vision of God in his temple: "One thing have I asked of the LORD, that will I seek after" (Ps 27:4). Scripture relates that several of the saints did, indeed, see God in his heavenly temple: Moses beholds of the form of God (Num 12:8), John reclines at Jesus' bosom (Jn 13:23), Stephen sees the glory of God (Acts 7:55), and Paul is caught up into the third heaven (2 Cor 12:2). Each of these saints contemplated God in his heavenly temple. And on the holy mountain, in Jesus' transfigured face, Peter, James, and John too witnessed heavenly glory. Contemplation takes us to Jesus, which is to say, it takes us into our heavenly destiny. Actions terminate in earthly objects, but contemplation terminates in heaven itself.[3] The unanimous witness of the Great Tradition, therefore, is that contemplation is greater than action. Saints often long for more contemplation, rarely for more action.

Only if we've been in heaven do we know how to live on earth. It is from the contemplative vision of truth that good action follows. The best action is a sharing of the fruits of one's contemplation. This is clear, for instance, from the episode that follows the transfiguration in Mark's Gospel. Immediately after narrating this account of supreme contemplation, Mark reports a story of action—or, rather, a story of failed action. The disciples are unable to cast out a boy's demon (Mk 9:18), which turns the narrative from the sublime to the ridiculous as the scribes argue with the disciples about why they cannot perform the exorcism (Mk 9:14). Jesus, whose face has just been shining with heavenly glory, responds to the father's plea for compassion (Mk 9:22). He heals the boy because it is his character to have compassion on crowds (see Mk 6:34; 8:2); on this occasion too, his compassion is directed toward "someone from the crowd" (Mk 9:17) as he tells

---

[3]See Michael Allen, *Grounded in Heaven: Recentering Christian Hope and Life on God* (Grand Rapids, MI: Eerdmans, 2018).

the deaf and mute spirit to come out (Mk 9:25). When the disciples afterward ask him privately why *they* couldn't cast it out, Jesus makes clear that this action requires prayer (Mk 9:29). It is clear that they have not spent time atop the mountain. What is true for them is true for us all: only with our face still shining with divine contemplation can we do acts of divine compassion.

Virtue is a topic of much discussion when it comes to theological interpretation.[4] This is as it should be, and I will turn to the topic of virtue in some detail in a moment. First, however, we should note that if the end determines the means, then it is primarily contemplation (not just virtue on its own) that shapes interpretation. Now, to be sure, I am convinced that virtue (and action) affects our interpretation too. But the summit and goal of the Christian life is contemplation, and so it is primarily contemplation of God in Christ that guides and shapes how we read the Scriptures.

Various forms of political reading have shaped both biblical and theological scholarship, particularly since Gustavo Gutiérrez's 1971 book *A Theology of Liberation*.[5] The Peruvian theologian issued a warning against separating church and politics, faith and economics. Gutiérrez argues that there is only one history: "There are not two histories, one profane and one sacred" but "only one human destiny, irreversibly assumed by Christ, the Lord of history."[6] The church's mission, therefore, is not to save people in the sense of "guaranteeing heaven."[7] Gutiérrez maintains that it is in this secular history that salvation happens (or not). Secularization, therefore, isn't just a move

---

[4]See, for instance, Stephen E. Fowl and L. Gregory Jones, *Reading in Communion: Scripture and Ethics in Christian Life* (Grand Rapids, MI: Eerdmans, 1991); Daniel J. Treier, *Virtue and the Voice of God: Toward Theology as Wisdom* (Grand Rapids, MI: Eerdmans, 2006); Richard Briggs, *The Virtuous Reader: Old Testament Narrative and Interpretive Virtue* (Grand Rapids, MI: Baker Academic, 2010).

[5]Gutiérrez's 1971 book was translated into English in 1973. Quotes are from *A Theology of Liberation: History, Politics, and Salvation*, rev. ed., trans. and ed. Caridad Inda and John Eagleson (Maryknoll, NY: Orbis, 1988).

[6]Gutiérrez, *Theology of Liberation*, 86.

[7]Gutiérrez, *Theology of Liberation*, 143.

away from the tutelage of religion and church, but it is also an encouraging sign that humanity is growing up by focusing on this-worldly salvation.[8] The God of the exodus is the God of history and of political liberation.[9] The exodus experience, Gutiérrez insists, remains paradigmatic for us today.[10] That is to say, Gutiérrez believes that the church has to look to the exodus and take it as an example of how to work for liberation of the oppressed in our time: "Peace, justice, love, and freedom are not private realities; they are not only internal attitudes. They are social realities, implying a historical liberation."[11]

In retrospect, liberation theology was merely the first obvious instance of the kind of contextual reading that has proliferated in biblical studies over the past number of decades. Today the field of biblical studies is chock-full of publications dealing with topics such as Paul and empire or the gospel and postcolonialism.[12] For the sake of illustration, let me mention just one example, Brian Walsh and Sylvia Keesmaat's *Colossians Remixed: Subverting the Empire*.[13] The book argues that the letter to the Colossians was "an explosive and subversive tract in the context of the Roman empire."[14] We are called to appropriate the letter's subversive imagination today, opposing as "alternative community" the (especially American) empire in all that we do. The consistent assumption is that gospel and empire are invariably and radically opposed—shades of gray are absent. The task

---

[8]Gutiérrez, *Theology of Liberation*, 42.

[9]Gutiérrez, *Theology of Liberation*, 89.

[10]Gutiérrez, *Theology of Liberation*, 90.

[11]Gutiérrez, *Theology of Liberation*, 97.

[12]See, e.g., Stephen D. Moore, *Empire and Apocalypse: Postcolonialism and the New Testament*, BMW 12 (Sheffield, UK: Sheffield Phoenix Press, 2006); Joerg Rieger, *Christ and Empire: From Paul to Postcolonial Times* (Minneapolis: Fortress, 2007); Scot McKnight and Joseph B. Modica, eds., *Jesus Is Lord, Caesar Is Not: Evaluating Empire in New Testament Studies* (Downers Grove, IL: IVP Academic, 2013); Kay Higuera Smith, Jayachitra Lalitha, and L. Daniel Hawk, eds., *Evangelical Postcolonial Conversations: Global Awakenings in Theology and Praxis* (Downers Grove, IL: IVP Academic, 2014).

[13]Brian J. Walsh and Sylvia C. Keesmaat, *Colossians Remixed: Subverting the Empire* (Downers Grove, IL: InterVarsity Press, 2004).

[14]Walsh and Keesmaat, *Colossians Remixed*, 7.

in the us-versus-them world of *Colossians Remixed*, therefore, is that
of defeating the empire—though not through violent means but by
sacrificial love.[15]

Walsh and Keesmaat's us-versus-them dualism is particularly troubling since one of the book's main aims is to oppose the exclusionary
violence of the empire. While the empire's violence is marked by
exclusion, the gospel breaks down "all ethnic, religious, social and
economic barriers."[16] But the authors don't actually think that inclusion, nonviolence, and hospitality are absolute. The repeated ac-
cusations of exclusion and violence in the direction of (American)
empire ring hollow considering the authors' own unwillingness to
embrace any kind of nuance in their evaluation. On their reading, the
limits of inclusion appear as soon as the empire comes into view.
Colossians, as a result, is consistently made to serve particular social
and political ends, not with a right-wing but with a left-wing agenda.[17]
My point here is not to express disagreement with the particulars of
Walsh and Keesmaat's social and political viewpoints—I actually
agree with quite a few of them. What's problematic is that the gospel
gets reduced to this-worldly ends.

A similar theological approach shapes the projects of Gutiérrez
and of Walsh and Keesmaat. Both treat sin and redemption primarily in this-worldly, structural terms. This is not to say that either
book ignores personal sin, but the overriding concern is with structural problems that oppress people and from which they must be
liberated. The theological projects are in the service of economic
and political goals, based on the underlying assumption that there
is only one history. But a this-worldly approach that focuses single-
mindedly on this-worldly problems and this-worldly solutions collapses Saint Paul's supernatural message into a natural, secular one.

---

[15]Walsh and Keesmaat, *Colossians Remixed*, 110.
[16]Walsh and Keesmaat, *Colossians Remixed*, 113.
[17]See, for instance, Walsh and Keesmaat, *Colossians Remixed*, 186-87.

William T. Cavanaugh puts his objection to Gutiérrez sharply but to the point: "The world has absorbed the church into itself."[18] Despite their prevailing us-versus-them approach (church-versus-empire), the same counts for Walsh and Keesmaat's commentary. Their denunciation of empire fails to convince, not because their criticism doesn't hold (which in many ways it does), but because like Gutiérrez they are unable to transcend this-worldly social realities. Their solutions remain on the horizontal timeline of politics and economics—which in practice simply means the exchange of right-wing with left-wing politics. In an important sense, therefore, the horizontal, this-worldly gospel of Gutiérrez and of Walsh and Keesmaat isn't radical enough. In Augustinian terms, because they don't reckon with the self-denying, vertical call of the heavenly City of God (*civitas Dei*), their politics remain restricted to the earthly city (*civitas terrena*). The empire isn't truly subverted.

The gospel involves a move from action to contemplation, from earth to heaven, from history to spirit. The Song of Moses in Exodus 15 certainly celebrates the defeat of Egypt. But we dare not forget that (1) the song itself emphatically treats this salvation as the result of supernatural intervention—it is the Lord who has shattered his enemies—so that salvation is not the result of Israel's economic or political action; and (2) Revelation 15 spiritualizes (dare I say, allegorizes) the historical victory over Egypt, so that a purely historical, this-worldly application of the exodus event would be far too restrictive. The heavenly saints stand beside the sea of glass, harps in hand, singing the song of Moses and of the Lamb (Rev 15:3). Saint John's apocalyptic vision transfigures and transcends the historical liberation from Egypt. This time it's not just one of its shadowy representations (such as Pharaoh) but it's the Beast itself that is defeated: freedom from sin is a spiritual reality first and foremost. The Red Sea

---

[18]William T. Cavanaugh, *Torture and Eucharist: Theology, Politics, and the Body of Christ* (Oxford: Blackwell, 1998), 180.

crossing corresponds to baptism, the wilderness journey to the Christian pilgrimage, manna to the Eucharist, and the earthly Jerusalem to the heavenly city.[19] In each case, the later spiritual reality is prefigured in the earlier physical type and (as the Fathers would have it) was already mystically present in it. Contemporary political readings fall short in their interpretive method: their reading of Scripture is flat, one-dimensional, this-worldly; what's lacking is a typological, spiritual reading of Scripture. The priority of heavenly contemplation over earthly action offers an important antidote to any unwarranted politicizing of the gospel.

PARTICIPATION IN VIRTUE

But the goal of contemplation does not devalue the active life. And, analogously, the aim of spiritual reading does not belittle literal interpretation. Saint Augustine recognized that we encounter Christ in our active life of caring for people in need and distress. "Don't be disappointed," he writes, "don't grumble because you were born at a time when you could not now see the Lord in the flesh. He hasn't, in fact, deprived you of this privilege and honor: *when you did it*, he says, *to one of the least of mine, you did it to me* (Mt 25:40)."[20] The active life is not to be despised. As Kimberly Baker rightly summarizes Augustine: "Martha's life has great value because she has the opportunity to serve Christ, an opportunity that extends to those who come after her because Christ continues to present himself to humanity through those in need."[21] Similarly, the literal meaning of the text, closely tied up with authorial intent, has great value. The *littera* contributes to our understanding of the *spiritus* and is indispensable as means to a greater end.

---

[19]See Jean Daniélou, *From Shadows to Reality: Studies in the Biblical Typology of the Fathers*, trans. Wulstan Hibberd (London: Burns & Oates, 1960), 153-66.

[20]Augustine, *Sermon* 103.2, in *Sermons*, ed. John E. Rotelle, trans. Edmund Hill, WSA III/4 (Brooklyn, NY: New City Press, 1992), 77.

[21]Baker, "Augustine," 35.

The fourth-century mystical theologian Gregory of Nyssa recognized this importance of the active life—not just the busy pastoral life of a priest or a bishop, but also the life of caring for the poor, the lepers, and the homeless. Gregory was the early church's most vigorous opponent of slavery, vehemently attacking what he regarded as an assault on people's physical freedom (*eleutheria*) and free will (*autexousia*). Berating slave owners in his preaching, Gregory chastises them:

> You have forgotten the limits of your authority, and that your rule is confined to control over things without reason. For it says *Let them rule over* winged creatures and four-footed things and creeping things (Gen, 1, 26). Why do you go beyond what is subject to you and raise yourself up against the very species which is free (*eleutheras*), counting your own kind on a level with four-footed things and even footless things?[22]

Gregory, rightly known for his contemplative mysticism and theology of ascent, regarded social justice as an integral part of the Christian life.[23]

Virtue is not a minor concern. In fact, for much of the Great Tradition, the lines between virtue (as the moral mode of the *vita activa*) and the *vita contemplativa* tend to blur. We see this in the way that Gregory discusses union with Christ. He speaks of Christ first of all as the aim of contemplation. When in *The Life of Moses* he talks about Moses stepping into the cloud of Mount Sinai (Ex 20:21), Gregory writes that Moses "slips into the inner sanctuary (*aduton*) of divine knowledge" and enters the "tabernacle not made with hands" (Heb 9:11).[24] Gregory identifies this heavenly tabernacle with Christ,

---

[22]Gregory of Nyssa, "Homily IV," in *Homilies on Ecclesiastes: An English Version with Supporting Studies—Proceedings of the Seventh International Colloquium on Gregory of Nyssa (St. Andrews, 5–10 September 1990)*, ed. Stuart George Hall (Berlin: de Gruyter, 1993), 73-74.

[23]For detailed discussion, see Hans Boersma, *Embodiment and Virtue in Gregory of Nyssa* (Oxford: Oxford University Press, 2013), 146-77.

[24]Gregory of Nyssa, *The Life of Moses*, trans. and ed. Abraham J. Malherbe and Everett Ferguson (Mahwah, NJ: Paulist Press, 1978), 2.167 (96).

uncreated in his preexistence,[25] and he speaks of the incarnate Christ (as well as of his church) as the earthly tabernacle.[26] When Moses reaches still higher and sees God's back from within a cleft on the rock (Ex 33:21-23), Gregory identifies the rock as Christ.[27] Similarly, in the Song of Songs, the bride's longing is always for Christ. He is the one the bride praises with the words, "Behold, you are beautiful, my kinsman, and glorious, in the shadow by our bed" (Song 1:16).[28] Christ as the groom is the one who is "not only beautiful (*kalos*), but the very essence of the Beautiful (*autē tou kalou hē ousia*)."[29] The bride's entry into the intelligible realm, explains Gregory, implies that "she is conformed to Christ, that she has recovered her very own beauty."[30] For Gregory, the goal of life is contemplation and divinization through union with Christ.

But Christ is not just the endpoint of contemplation.[31] Gregory speaks of Christ also as the very definition of virtue. He makes this point explicitly in *On What It Means to Call Oneself a Christian*, insisting that in Christ all of the virtues are one. He then adds: "If we, who are united to Him by faith in Him are joined (*synaptomenoi*) to Him whose incorruptible nature is beyond verbal interpretation, it is entirely necessary for us to become what is contemplated in connection with that incorruptible nature and to achieve identity with the secondary elements which follow along with it. For just as by participating (*metochē*) in Christ we are given the title 'Christian,' so also are we drawn into a share in the lofty ideas which it implies."[32] We

---

[25]Gregory of Nyssa, *Life of Moses* 2.74 (98).

[26]Gregory of Nyssa, *Life of Moses* 2.174-75; 2.184 (98-99, 101).

[27]Gregory of Nyssa, *Life of Moses* 2.244 (117).

[28]I quote the Song of Songs from the translation of Gregory's own use of the Greek text, as found in Gregory of Nyssa, *Homilies on the Song of Songs*, trans. and ed. Richard A. Norris, Writings from the Greco-Roman World 13 (Atlanta: Society of Biblical Literature, 2012).

[29]Gregory of Nyssa, *Homilies on the Song of Songs* 4.107 (119).

[30]Gregory of Nyssa, *Homilies on the Song of Songs* 15.440 (467).

[31]The following two paragraphs draw from Hans Boersma, *Embodiment and Virtue*, 221-28.

[32]Gregory of Nyssa, *On What It Means to Call Oneself a Christian*, in *Ascetical Works*, trans. Virginia Woods Callahan, FC 58 (Washington, DC: Catholic University Press of America, 1967), 84; translation adjusted.

become what we contemplate, according to Gregory, by sharing in Christ. And for Gregory, this is the same as sharing in virtue. Christ is capital-V Virtue, and we participate in him by joining him through our own lives of virtue.

Saint Gregory makes this point in a poignant manner in his book *On Perfection*. Here he links capital-V Virtue with Christ—as well as with perfection. Gregory discusses the numerous biblical names for Christ in Scripture, and he insists that it is our life of virtue that gives us a share in these names. So, if we want to be Christians, Gregory insists, we must live up to our name: "Being something does not result from being called something."[33] In other words, we participate in Christ (and so are Christians) if and when we participate in Virtue itself by means of our thoughts, words, and actions.[34] Comparing human virtue to water in a jar drawn from a stream, Gregory comments: "Drawing from Him as from a pure and uncorrupted stream, a person will show in his thoughts such a resemblance to his Prototype as exists between the water in the running water or stream and the water taken away from there in a jar. For the purity in Christ and the purity seen in the person who has a share (*metochoi*) in Him are the same, the One being the stream and the other drawn from it."[35] For Gregory, the life of virtue itself constitutes our sharing or participating in Christ. Obviously, this is a far cry from the *sola fide* of the Reformation. But it is not, for that, any less Christ centered. For Gregory, the life of virtue is a life of participation in Christ.

This close identification of virtue with Christ implies a blurring of the lines between action and contemplation. Gregory contrasts the old man (Adam) with the new man (Christ), arguing along with Saint Paul that we are to take off Adam as the old man and instead put on Christ as the new man (see Eph 4:22-24; Col 3:9-10). Just as these

---

[33]Gregory of Nyssa, *On Perfection*, in *Ascetical Works*, trans. Virginia Woods Callahan, FC 58 (Washington, DC: Catholic University Press of America, 1967), 98.

[34]Gregory of Nyssa, *On Perfection*, 120.

[35]Gregory of Nyssa, *On Perfection*, 121.

Pauline passages link the old man with vices and the new man with virtues, so also Gregory focuses on the moral change of the believer. He begins his first homily on the Song of Songs as follows:

> You who in accordance with the counsel of Paul have "taken off" the old humanity with its deeds and lusts like a filthy garment (*peribolaion*) (Col 3:9) and have clothed yourselves by purity of life in the lightsome raiment (*himatia*) of the Lord, raiment such as he revealed in his transfiguration on the mountain (cf. Mark 9:2-3 and par.), or, rather, you who have "put on" our Lord Jesus Christ himself (Gal 3:27) together with his holy garb (*stolēs*) and with him have been transfigured for impassibility and the life divine: hear the mysteries of the Song of Songs.[36]

For Gregory, to take off the old man is to leave behind a life of vice, while to put on the new man is to embark on a life of virtue. The clothing metaphor implied in the expressions *taking off* and *putting on* held particular appeal to Gregory because he identified Adam and Eve's "garments of skin" (Gen 3:21) with the fallen human condition. So, the way to get rid of the tunics of hide (the fallen life of the passions) is to replace them with the "holy garb" of Christ (the life of virtue).[37] For Gregory, then, Christ is the focal point both of virtue and of contemplation. The reason it's sometimes hard to distinguish the two is that both are centered on participation in Christ.

Of course, Saint Peter makes the same point: the more virtuous we become, the more our character reflects that of God. Few biblical passages are as direct in establishing this link between virtue and divinization as 2 Peter 1:3-11. Saint Peter addresses here the *vita activa*—"all things that pertain to life and godliness" (2 Pet 1:3). Three times he uses the term *aretē* or "virtue" (2 Pet 1:3, 5). The first time, the ESV translates *aretē* as "excellence": we are called to God's

---

[36]Gregory of Nyssa, *Homilies on the Song of Songs* 1.14-15 (15).
[37]I discuss Gregory's use of the clothing metaphor in detail in *Embodiment and Virtue*, 87-92.

own "glory and excellence." The other two times, the ESV has the term *virtue*. I prefer consistency in translation, but having two terms, *virtue* and *excellence*, side by side, both translating the same Greek word, is nonetheless striking. It's a reminder that for Peter, as for the Greek tradition preceding the New Testament, virtue is a practice or a skill at which we can become good, even excellent, if we keep at it, much like we hone our skill in the game of chess by continuously playing it.

When he goes on to discuss the virtues in more detail, the apostle lists eight of them: faith, virtue, knowledge, self-control, steadfastness, godliness, brotherly affection, and love.[38] It is noteworthy that Peter lists seven items plus one. Seven often denotes the fullness of created life, beginning with the seven (*sheva*) creation days that culminate in Sabbath (*shabbat*). Peter adds to the seven virtues the virtue of love, which takes us into the eighth day of the resurrection and eternal life. The greatest virtue, which continues into eternity, is love. And, for Saint Augustine at least, we would not go wrong in treating all of the virtues of our earthly life as sharing in some way in the perfection of eternal love. As he discusses the four cardinal virtues, the bishop of Hippo links them to love:

> If virtue leads us to the happy life, then I would not define virtue in any other way than as the perfect love of God. For in speaking of virtue as fourfold, one refers, as I understand it, to the various dispositions of love itself. Therefore, these four virtues—would that their efficacy were present in all souls as their names are on all lips—I would not hesitate to define as follows: temperance is love giving itself wholeheartedly to that which is loved, fortitude is love enduring all things willingly for the sake of that which is loved, justice is love serving alone that which is loved

---

[38]Peter is so keen on highlighting the significance of "virtue" that he uses it both as a broader, all-encompassing term and as one of the eight.

and thus ruling rightly, and prudence is love choosing wisely between that which helps it and that which hinders it.[39]

Virtue, for Augustine, is the perfect love of God, which in turn is the perfection of temperance, fortitude, justice, and prudence. Similarly, for Saint Peter, virtue is the perfect love of God, which in turn is the perfection of his list of seven virtues.

Moreover, Saint Peter does not treat the list of virtues in moralistic fashion as a purely external list of obligations one has to meet. Rather, these virtues are a sharing in God's "own (*idia*) glory and excellence" (2 Pet 1:3). Human virtue or excellence is participation in divine virtue or excellence. This is why Peter links progress in the practice of virtue with divinization: we become "partakers of the divine nature" (*theias koinōnoi physeōs*) and escape the "corruption" (*phthoras*) that stems from "sinful desire" (*epithymia*; 2 Pet 1:4). The apostle links mortality or corruption with sin; to escape it, therefore, is to become immortal, like God (see 1 Cor 15:50-55). Or, we could also say, when we become divine in virtue, we end up participating also in divine immortality.

Peter thinks of this divinization as transfiguration. We are called, he claims, to God's own "glory (*doxē*) and excellence" (2 Pet 1:3). Peter had been an "eyewitness" (2 Pet 1:16) to the transfiguration "on the holy mountain" (2 Pet 1:18). He had seen the honor, glory, and majesty of Christ—the same as that of the "Majestic Glory" of the Father (2 Pet 1:17). In other words, when through a life of virtue we participate in God's glory and virtue, we are transported, as it were, to the Mount of Transfiguration and, like Peter, James, and John, are enabled to see the divine light of immortality. Virtue conforms us to the transfigured Christ—to his virtue and his glory. The ultimate aim is contemplation and divinization. Virtue is the intermediate aim, as it unites us to the character of God.

[39]Augustine of Hippo, *The Catholic and Manichaean Ways of Life*, ed. Roy Joseph Deferrari, trans. Donald A. Gallagher and Idella J. Gallagher, FC 56 (Washington, DC: Catholic University of America Press, 1966), 15.25 (22).

FROM VIRTUE TO INTERPRETATION

If virtue serves contemplation, then we must ask the question of how virtue relates to biblical interpretation. After all, the final end of both virtue and biblical interpretation is contemplation of God. The first (and culturally counterintuitive) point to make in this regard is that our actions—and in particular the moral manner or mode (*tropos* in Greek) in which we perform them—affect our interpretation of Scripture. It's not just the case that we ought to read Scripture with an eye to moral implications, though of course there is such a thing as a moral reading of Scripture, traditionally referred to as "tropology." But it is also that our moral lives in turn shape the way we read Scripture. In other words, we should pay attention not just to what Stephen Fowl calls "virtue-through-interpretation" (reading the Bible with a view to virtuous action) but also to what he calls "virtue-in-interpretation" (virtuous lives leading to good interpretation).[40]

A little side-tour into Alisdair MacIntyre may be helpful here.[41] In his book *After Virtue*, MacIntyre suggests that all we have left of the moral life in our society is fragments. He calls them "simulacra of morality."[42] The problem, as MacIntyre points out, is that to reach our telos we need moral practices (virtues) that are in line with it. These practices, explains MacIntyre, yield goods that are integral (or internal) to the practices themselves. He offers chess as an example of a practice whose goods are internal to the game: "There are the goods internal to the practice of chess which cannot be had in any way but by playing chess or some other game of that specific kind. We call them internal for two reasons: first . . . because we can only specify them in terms of chess or some other game of that specific kind and by means of examples from such games . . . and secondly because they

---

[40]Stephen E. Fowl, "Virtue," in *DTIB*, 837-39.

[41]For an insightful lengthier discussion of the connection between MacIntyre's virtue ethics and biblical interpretation, see Briggs, *Virtuous Reader*, 21-39.

[42]Alasdair MacIntyre, *After Virtue: A Study in Moral Theory*, 3rd ed. (Notre Dame, IN: University of Notre Dame Press, 2007), 2.

can only be identified and recognized by the experience of participating in the practice in question. Those who lack the relevant experience are incompetent thereby as judges of internal goods."[43] For
MacIntyre, virtues are particular, communal practices that enable
those participating in them to achieve their internal goods.

MacIntyre, a convert from Marxism to Christianity, is a key figure
in the retrieval of virtue ethics. He emphasizes that the moral life has
to do more with character than with rules. To be sure, Christian morality does involve law and rules (some of them absolute in character).
But the rules are not alien to us—they fit with how God has created
us, which means that by living up to them we bend or shape our lives
to be in line with the final heavenly telos. The more we live in line
with our heavenly telos, the happier we are. Moral rules do come from
God (so that in some sense they are external to us), but they are in
line with the telos that is already embedded within us (and so is internal to us). This means that the morality of our actions is always
more than mere adherence to rules. Morality is, instead, the shaping
of our character in accordance both with our created identity and
with our final end. Just as it is only by playing chess that we get the
pay-off of the game (e.g., learning strategic planning, intellectual
stimulation, conviviality, and perhaps even scoring a win), so too it
is only by living virtuously that we reach our heavenly goal.

MacIntyre's point has implications for biblical interpretation. As
long as we read the Bible without the Spirit of God, we're not truly
interpreting Scripture. We may gain certain insights, but we don't
grasp the aim itself to which the biblical passages are meant to guide
us. As long as we don't participate, through the Spirit, in the virtue or
excellence (*aretē*) or God, we won't be able to grasp the practice of
biblical interpretation. Skillful biblical interpretation is something
we learn by living skillfully or virtuously. (And, in turn, as we learn

---

[43]MacIntyre, *After Virtue*, 188-89.

to read Scripture better, this makes us more virtuous.) Stephen Fowl
puts it this way as he discusses what he calls "virtue-in-interpretation":
"It simply stands to reason that those who have advanced in the
Christian life will tend to offer the best interpretations."[44] Why?
Divine lives grasp divine things. Put in Saint Paul's own words, "The
natural person does not accept the things of the Spirit of God, for
they are folly to him, and he is not able to understand them because
they are spiritually discerned" (1 Cor 2:14). God, who is perfect in
glory and virtue, knows all things and as such grasps even the greatest
depths of the divine Scriptures. As their author, he knows them fully
and comprehensively. The more we are transfigured to participate in
God's glory and virtue, the more we, too, grasp the depths of the
divine Scriptures. Recall MacIntyre's words: the internal goods of a
practice "can only be identified and recognized by the experience of
participating in the practice in question." Only by participating in the
excellence (*aretē*) of God do we begin to learn what excellence (*aretē*)
in biblical interpretation looks like in practice. Christian living and
interpretation both require virtue in order to arrive at the God who
is Virtue itself. The best Christians are the best Bible readers.

It stands to reason, then, that charity or love, the greatest of the
virtues, makes for the best interpretations. In his book *On Christian
Doctrine*, Saint Augustine elaborates on charity as a rule for interpretation. He begins his discussion of interpretation by speaking of
Christ as both the endpoint and the road of the journey.[45] After all,
he is "the way, and the truth, and the life" (Jn 14:6), which Augustine
takes to mean "you come *by* me, you come *to* me, you abide *in* me."[46]
If Christ is both the road and the endpoint, this implies that he is the
one we meet in the Scriptures (as the way) as well as the one to whom
the Scriptures point (as the truth). Christ, after all, is the end of the

---

[44]Fowl, "Virtue," 838.

[45]Augustine, *On Christian Teaching*, trans. and ed. R. P. H. Green (Oxford: Oxford University
Press, 1997), 1.34.38 (26); emphasis added.

[46]Augustine, *On Christian Teaching* 1.34.38 (26).

law (Rom 10:4). For Augustine, as for Paul, to say that Christ is the end of the law is the same as saying that love is the end of the law (Rom 13:10). And so the bishop treats both Christ and love as the end or purpose of reading Scripture, commenting: "So anyone who thinks that he has understood the divine scriptures or any part of them, but cannot by his understanding build up this double love of God and neighbor, has not yet succeeded in understanding them."[47] Love (which for Augustine is the same as the heavenly enjoyment of God in Christ) is the purpose of Scripture, and so to arrive at love is to arrive at Scripture's telos.

So much is this the case that Augustine insists that someone who is truly loving no longer needs the Scriptures: "A person strengthened by faith, hope, and love, and who steadfastly holds on to them, has no need of the scriptures except to instruct others."[48] The Scriptures, for Augustine, are a sacrament or means of grace. Once the *res* (the fullness of love or Christ himself) has manifested itself, the *sacramentum* (the Scriptures) become superfluous. Of course, those of us who still struggle with the theological virtues do need to immerse ourselves in Scripture, for it is Scripture that makes us more loving. As Alan Jacobs puts it, "Augustine is inscribing a kind of hermeneutical circle here: readers must read lovingly in order to receive the biblical message of love, but the more clearly they receive that message, the more lovingly they will be able to read."[49] Jacobs's hermeneutical circle articulates what I mentioned earlier: that our moral lives shape and are shaped by the way we read Scripture.

Saint Augustine was not indifferent to authorial intent. He explains that sometimes we arrive at an interpretation that "differs from that of the writer" and so are misled.[50] We may still reach the end goal (love or Christ), but we are "like a walker who leaves his path by mistake

[47]Augustine, *On Christian Teaching* 1.36.40 (27).
[48]Augustine, *On Christian Teaching* 1.39.43 (28).
[49]Alan Jacobs, "Love," in *DTIB*, 466.
[50]Augustine, *On Christian Teaching* 1.36.41 (27).

but reaches the destination to which the path leads by going through a field."[51] Augustine figures it's best not to leave the path and to arrive at the endpoint of love without first going astray. Authorial intent does enter into the overall configuration of how to interpret Scripture.

Still, we should not absolutize Augustine's comments here. First, his own exegesis is generally incredibly playful (think, for instance, of his interpretation of Ps 73:28, which I discussed in the previous chapter), so that it is hard to imagine Augustine holding to authorial intent with unbending rigor. Authorial intent wasn't as straightforward a notion for Augustine as it tends to be for modern readers. In book twelve of his *Confessions*, Augustine expresses impatience with those who think their interpretation is precisely what Moses intended.[52] Scholars have suggested, therefore, that Augustine was likely open to polyvalent meanings, even at the literal level; it may not be possible to pin down the sacred authors to just one subjective intention.[53] Numerous different readings may cohere with the one divine truth. Second, for Augustine, human and divine intent were much more closely interwoven than they tend to be for us moderns. His strong commitment to divine providence (and his understanding of biblical authors as inspired prophets) means that it was easy for him to place human intent in the service of (the more important) divine intent.[54] Repeatedly, Augustine insists that the patriarchs,

---

[51]Augustine, *On Christian Teaching* 1.36.41 (27).

[52]Augustine, *Confessions*, trans. and ed. Henry Chadwick (Oxford: Oxford University Press, 1991), 12.31.42 (270-71).

[53]See the discussion in Carol Harrison, "'Not Words but Things': Harmonious Diversity in the Four Gospels," in *Augustine: Biblical Exegete*, ed. Frederick Van Fleteren and Joseph C. Schnaubelt (New York: Lang, 2001), 167-70.

[54]Tarmo Toom explains that Augustine did not take human authorial intent as the ultimate interpretive criterion, both out of concern for the priority of divine intent and in order to safeguard a christological reading of the Old Testament ("Was Augustine an Intentionalist? Authorial Intention in Augustine's Hermeneutics," *SP* 70 [2013]: 186-89). Toom comments: "What ultimately mattered was what God intended to say to the hearers of the Word at any time and place, rather than what human co-authors wanted to say to their immediate audiences. Augustine simply refused to keep the meaning of a text frozen exclusively to its particular historical and cultural location of origin" (Toom, "Was Augustine an Intentionalist?," 187).

prophets, and Old Testament authors knew of the spiritual (divinely intended) meaning of their message.[55] Finally, for Augustine the human author of Scripture always aims at love, and so if our interpretation does not promote love, we have not properly understood him. The supreme rule, Augustine contends, is the rule of charity: "So when someone has learnt that the aim of the commandment is 'love from a pure heart, and good conscience and genuine faith' [1 Tim. 1:5], he will be ready to relate every interpretation of the holy scriptures to these three things and may approach the task of handling these books with confidence."[56] We learn confidence in exegesis not primarily by acquiring scientific tools but by learning to love well.

It is difficult for us moderns to appreciate that biblical interpretation depends more on virtue (love) than on scientific tools. We typically think of exegesis as an exercise in mapping the DNA of the surface of the text rather than as an exploration of an enchanted forest that holds ever-deeper mysteries. The reason for this is metaphysical. I dealt with metaphysics in chapter two ("No Plato, No Scripture"), and I won't go back to it here in any detail. But I do need to make one important point: for the Christian Platonism of the Great Tradition, both virtue and exegesis are about participation. Both allow us to enter into and explore the infinite "forest" of the divine mystery; both lead us deeper into the infinite goodness of God. The doctrine of participation assumes that nature and the supernatural are closely linked. By contrast, modernity, by bracketing out God, has radically separated nature and the supernatural. On this understanding, nature is always *just* nature. It's always *pure* nature. The outcome? Virtue

---

[55]Examples of this abound in Augustine's corpus. See, e.g., Augustine, *On Christian Teaching* 3.9.13 (75); 3.27.38 (87); *Answer to Faustus, a Manichean*, ed. Boniface Ramsey, trans. Roland Teske, WSA I (Hyde Park, NY: New City Press, 2007), 16.23 (20:216); *The First Catechetical Instruction*, ed. Johannes Quasten and Joseph C. Plumpe, trans. Joseph P. Christopher, ACW 2 (New York: Newman Press, 1947), 3.6 (20); *Expositions of the Psalms: 73–98*, ed. John E. Rotelle, trans. Maria Boulding, WSA III (Hyde Park, NY: New City Press, 2002), 18:91.
[56]Augustine, *On Christian Teaching* 1.40.44 (29); square brackets original.

becomes a purely natural thing, which we somehow have to conjure up ourselves (which is why we moderns are Pelagian by inclination). The biblical text, too, becomes a purely natural thing, whose DNA we try to map through scientific analysis.

Unlike many modern biblical scholars, the church fathers' focus was not the surface of the text. Their exegesis was not a matter of mapping the DNA. Instead, they were interested in tracing how the text may conform us to Christ. Scripture, in patristic exegesis, serves the purpose of participating in heaven—in Christ, that is. Exegesis, therefore, was primarily mystagogical rather than scientific in character. That is to say, Scripture served as a spiritual guide facilitating one's entry into the divine life. Rather than empirically trying to figure out the details of the literal meaning of the text, the church fathers encourage us to look for ways in which Scripture can serve its divinely intended function of conforming us to Christ and thereby allowing us eternally to contemplate him.

CONCLUSION

Theologically, we are in dire need of recovering otherworldliness. It is hardly a coincidence that the rise of historical-biblical scholarship has gone hand in hand with a neglect of topics such as contemplation, heaven, and the vision of God. When we make the historical angle the primary one (perhaps even the only one) in our reading of the Bible, the inevitable result is that this-worldly, natural realities take center stage. Those historical realities were not the primary focus of the Old Testament authors; they focused first and foremost on the face of God: "Seek the Lord and his strength; seek his presence continually!" (Ps 105:4). Nor was historical reconstruction the central exegetical concern of the New Testament authors when they turned to the Scriptures. Their use of the Old Testament had to do with usefulness (*ōpheleia*) more than with reconstruction. Seen in this light, the church fathers' use of Scripture is very much in line with that of the New Testament's use of the Old, while the exegetical approaches of modern biblical scholarship are, for the most part, widely off-course. The main difference is that both the biblical authors and the church fathers were contemplative in their concerns, while the historicism of modernity is this-worldly in orientation.

As I have made clear in this chapter, it is not as though we should shun this-worldly concerns. They have their rightful place. After all, in much of this chapter I have focused on the *vita activa* from the angle of virtue. But we approach the active life rightly only when we recognize that it results from heavenly contemplation and in turn aims at heavenly contemplation. The increasing emphasis on social justice, as witnessed for example in political readings of the New Testament, focuses on action to the exclusion of contemplation. By contrast, for the church fathers, virtue itself was already a participation in the life of God, and so the *vita activa* was not opposed to contemplation but served it. The risk of the contemporary focus on social justice and on political and economic readings of Scripture is that they remain on the surface. In Augustinian terms, such readings of Scripture don't distinguish between using (*uti*) temporal, created things and enjoying (*frui*) the triune God himself.[57] The Great Tradition rightly recognized that in theological exegesis, we move from history to spirit, so as to align our reading of Scripture with the ultimate aim of contemplating God in Christ.

The real issue underlying each of the five chapters of this book is that of love. In interpretation, the rule of love (*regula caritatis*) distinguishes right from wrong. When we treat biblical exegesis as a historical discipline, we separate the biblical text from its divinely intended telos of heavenly contemplation—the love of God in Christ. By positing a purely natural reading of the text—even if it's only a

---

[57]Augustine's *On Christian Teaching* is basically a treatise responding to the question "whether humans should enjoy one another or use one another, or both." *On Christian Teaching* 1.12.20 (16).

methodological naturalism that we pursue—we separate the biblical text as a human document from the supernatural aim of loving God. In other words, the modern lack of a participatory view of reality obscures the spiritual purpose of the biblical text, and we end up treating it (methodologically at least) with naturalist presuppositions. To put it bluntly: historical interpretation doesn't require a relationship with God.

Of course, many biblical scholars will argue that they are not losing sight of the spiritual concerns because they deal with them in the application that follows exegesis. But this still treats exegesis itself as a purely historical affair. By separating application from exegesis, this approach abandons the participatory understanding of the exegetical endeavor that marked the Great Tradition. As we saw in Gregory of Nyssa, the earlier tradition maintained that from the outset interpretation of the biblical text aims at the renewal of our lives in Christ. Virtue (or, in pastoral-theological parlance, application) is not a supernatural building block added on top of a purely natural foundation. Rather, Virtue is Christ, and from the outset the real interpretive concern is how to participate more fully in his heavenly life.

We need to recover a contemplative mode of reading Scripture—a reading that puts the entire exegetical practice in the service of the love of God in Christ. We need to relearn that the telos determines the means. The Bible cannot be read apart from its spiritual end, which is the heavenly contemplation of God in Christ. When we do so anyway, we blind ourselves to Scripture's final cause (the heavenly presence of God) and lose its divine character. It is contemplative reading that puts us in sync with the purposes of God. No heaven, no Scripture.

CONCLUSION

ACADEMIC SPECIALIZATION BRINGS both gains and losses. It usually means greater understanding within a narrower field of knowledge; it also typically means less understanding of other fields of study, even areas that may be related to one's own. A similar tally of pros and cons holds true for specialization in theological studies. Without doubt, the separation of biblical and dogmatic theology yields benefits to both. In terms of gains, the isolation of biblical studies from dogmatic theology has offered numerous insights into the historical backdrop of the biblical writings. As a result, contemporary biblical scholars work with a knowledge pool that was simply unavailable to premodern students of Scripture.

My contention in this book, however, is that the gains do not outweigh the losses. For one, I am not sure that it's possible to pinpoint a gain for dogmatic theology in its separation from biblical theology. Dogmatic theology merely loses out when it gets isolated from Scripture. But biblical theology, too, suffers when separated from dogmatic concerns. In fact, biblical theology isn't biblical at all when it treats exegesis primarily as a historical discipline, taking no account of theological considerations in its interpretation of the text. Indeed, the problem is usually worse for biblical than for dogmatic theology: many biblical scholars take it as their task to read the biblical text without theological presuppositions or ends, while no dogmatic theologian would dream of engaging in doing theology without taking Scripture as norm or guide of some kind.

Throughout this book, I have made the point that a *purely* biblical theology—that is, a theology grounded in *pura scriptura*—ends up undermining the very edifice it attempts to safeguard. The edifice I have in mind is the centrality of the Scriptures for the Christian life. When we focus on Scripture apart from Christ, whose presence in both Old and New Testaments is the reason the church claims them, we lose our most significant reason for reading it, namely, to find Christ. When we employ a hermeneutic that fails to focus on Christ, Scripture can no longer build up the faith of the church, which is focused on Christ, and wherever Christians buy into such a non-christological reading of Scripture, Scripture ends up losing its grip on their lives.

Similarly, when we try to read Scripture apart from any metaphysical presuppositions whatsoever, our very attempt to exalt the Bible collapses in on itself. Faith isn't meant to function without reason, and we shouldn't attempt to do theology without philosophy. The isolation of Scripture vis-à-vis metaphysics is practically impossible: invariably it means the unwitting adoption of one metaphysic or another—most of the time one that assumes nominalist presuppositions since they make up the metaphysical air that we breathe and make our own metaphysic without us even being aware of it. When we try to isolate Scripture from metaphysical presuppositions, we make it the unsuspecting victim of whatever philosophy happens to be prevalent. It seems far more prudent to acknowledge the potential benefit of metaphysics and to ask which metaphysical account coheres with what we find in Scripture.

Scripture similarly suffers when we read the Bible like any other book—ignoring that God in his providence has given us this book for a particular purpose, namely, to lead us into his presence. The confession of divine providence, therefore, precludes a hermeneutic that simply asks the historical question of authorial intent. Within God's providence, Scripture serves not primarily to point us back to the historical meaning(s) but to lead us forward toward eternal life. Any hermeneutic that claims that we are supposed to recover the one, true meaning of the text by means of historical analysis fails to take into account what it is that turns these particular writings into Scripture. They are Scripture because of God's gracious, Christ-shaped providential purposes with our lives. It is impossible to explain to ordinary Christians why they should read the Bible if their understanding of it is first and foremost a historical rather than a spiritual matter. The lively, existential reading of Scripture by believers invariably withers in a context that keeps reinforcing the erroneous notion that Scripture is an object that we can properly grasp only when we have access to the proper scientific scholarly apparatus.

Scripture, therefore, is best read within the church, not the academy. I am not suggesting that linguists, archeologists, and historians cannot shed light on the meaning of the text. Nor do I mean to imply that scholarly training is problematic or out of place. It is true, after all, that the *relative* independence of nature vis-à-vis grace means that it is possible to come to some genuine understanding of linguistic and historical issues without faith in Christ. But the caveats on this acknowledgment are twofold. First, the Christian knows that scientific (as well as historical) insights are never a matter of *pure* science or *pure* history. One's confession of faith in Christ properly embeds or encapsulates scientific and historical claims. There is no such thing as a *pura natura* and, therefore, no such thing as strict independence of historical claims in relation to the Christian faith. Historical exegesis may never adopt methodological naturalism; it must always take account of the supernatural presuppositions of the Spirit as Scripture's primary author and of the church as the community of faith within which the Bible takes on meaning.

Second, linguists, archeologists, and historians—precisely inasmuch as they limit themselves to their academic field of study—typically do not ask themselves the question of the purpose of Scripture. By contrast, the church constantly deals with the question of the purpose of the Bible. After all, the church is the "pillar and buttress of the truth" (1 Tim 3:15), and it is the church's task to safeguard and pass on the truth of the Scriptures so that they may continue in their role of assisting people in safely crossing the Jordan River into the Promised Land. Of course, the church should take into account scholarly exegetical insights. But if Scripture functions as a means of grace through which we are nurtured into God's eternal kingdom, then it is the church, not the academy, that offers the more definitive context for biblical interpretation.

The purpose of Scripture is to bring us to heaven. When we ignore the latter, we end up demoting also the former. Both the active and the contemplative life are indispensable to holistic Christian living; yet, it is not the active but the contemplative life that is our ultimate aim. There is no higher aim than to see God in Christ. Talk about heaven, therefore, is not talk about some far-away place. It is, instead, talk about the happiness that awaits us in the joyful, face-to-face meeting with God in Christ. When biblical exegesis loses sight of such heavenly concerns and instead focuses on earthly transformation, it sends the subliminal message that it is just fine to set our minds on earthly things alone (see Phil 3:19). But why read Scripture if, concerned to make this world a better place, we ignore its deepest aim? God has made us such that only by contemplating his presence in Christ do we experience true happiness. A biblical hermeneutic that fails to recognize this (by focusing instead on political or social improvements) fails to understand human beings' deepest desire. It doesn't take long for churches that focus on action rather than contemplation to empty out. Why? Scripture has lost its proper place as a sacrament leading to eternal life.

If there's one thing I wish biblical scholars knew (and, really, not just biblical scholars, but all who read the Bible), it is that the Bible is a sacrament. It is one of God's key means of grace leading us to eternal life. When we treat the Bible as our ultimate object of devotion, we change its function from that of sacrament (*sacramentum*) to that of reality (*res*). Simply put, we idolize it. By doing so, we forget the kinds of things that help us read Scripture well—Christology, metaphysics, providence, church, and heaven. Each of these five elements helps us treat Scripture as a God-given sacrament. Isolating Scripture from the spiritual end for which it is meant does not put it on a pedestal (no matter our intentions) but instead diminishes it and opens it up to manipulation and abuse. Only when we acknowledge Holy Scripture's proper *pen*-ultimacy as divine sacrament will it serve to bring to fruition the ultimate rule of the eternal love of God in Christ.

BIBLIOGRAPHY

Allen, Michael. *Grounded in Heaven: Recentering Christian Hope and Life on God.* Grand Rapids, MI: Eerdmans, 2018.

Allert, Craig D. *A High View of Scripture? The Authority of the Bible and the Formation of the New Testament Canon.* Grand Rapids, MI: Baker Academic, 2007.

Anderson, Garwood P. *Paul's New Perspective: Charting a Soteriological Journey.* Downers Grove, IL: IVP Academic, 2016.

Antonova, Stamenka. "Providence." In *The Westminster Handbook to Origen*, edited by John Anthony McGuckin, 181-82. Louisville, KY: Westminster John Knox, 2004.

Athanasius. *Four Discourses Against the Arians.* In NPNF 2/4.

Augustine. *Answer to Faustus, a Manichean.* Edited by Boniface Ramsey. Translated by Roland Teske. WSA I/20. Hyde Park, NY: New City Press, 2007.

——. *The Catholic and Manichaean Ways of Life.* Edited by Roy Joseph Deferrari. Translated by Donald A. Gallagher and Idella J. Gallagher. FC 56. Washington, DC: Catholic University of America Press, 1966.

——. *Confessions.* Translated and edited by Henry Chadwick. Oxford: Oxford University Press, 1991.

——. *Expositions of the Psalms: 73–98.* Edited by John E. Rotelle. Translated by Maria Boulding. WSA III/18. Hyde Park, NY: New City Press, 2002.

——. *The First Catechetical Instruction.* Edited by Johannes Quasten and Joseph C. Plumpe. Translated by Joseph P. Christopher. ACW 2. New York: Newman Press, 1947.

——. *The Letter and the Spirit.* In *Augustine: Later Works.* Translated and edited by John Burnaby. LCC 8. Philadelphia: Westminster John Knox, 1955.

——. *On Christian Teaching.* Translated and edited by R. P. H. Green. Oxford: Oxford University Press, 1997.

——. *Sermons.* Edited by John E. Rotelle. Translated by Edmund Hill. WSA III/4 and III/5. Brooklyn, NY: New City Press, 1992.

Ayres, Lewis. *Nicaea and Its Legacy: An Approach to Fourth-Century Trinitarian Theology*. Oxford: Oxford University Press, 2004.

Baker, David L. *Two Testaments, One Bible: The Theological Relationship Between the Old and New Testaments*. 3rd ed. Downers Grove, IL: InterVarsity Press, 2010.

Baker, Kimberly F. "Augustine on Action, Contemplation, and Their Meeting Point in Christ." PhD diss., University of Notre Dame, 2007.

Balthasar, Hans Urs von, ed. *Origen: Spirit and Fire—A Thematic Anthology of His Writings*. Translated by Robert J. Daly. Washington, DC: Catholic University of America Press, 1984.

———. "Theology and Sanctity." In *The Word Made Flesh*, vol. 1 of *Explorations in Theology*, translated by A. V. Littledale with Alexander Dru, 181-209. San Francisco: Ignatius, 1989.

Behr, John. *The Nicene Faith*. Vol. 2 of *The Formation of Christian Theology*. Crestwood, NY: St. Vladimir's Seminary Press, 2001.

———. *The Way to Nicaea*. Vol. 1 of *The Formation of Christian Theology*. Crestwood, NY: St. Vladimir's Seminary Press, 2001.

Bingham, D. Jeffrey. *Irenaeus' Use of Matthew's Gospel in* Adversus Haereses. TEG 7. Leuven: Peeters, 1998.

Blackwell, Ben C. "Paul and Irenaeus." In *Paul and the Second Century: The Legacy of Paul's Life, Letters, and Teaching*, edited by Michael F. Bird and Joseph R. Dodson, 190-206. LNTS 412. New York: T&T Clark, 2011.

Boersma, Hans. *Embodiment and Virtue in Gregory of Nyssa: An Anagogical Approach*. Oxford: Oxford University Press, 2013.

———. "Justification Within Recapitulation: Irenaeus in Ecumenical Dialogue." *IJST* 22 (2020): 169-90.

———. *Nouvelle Théologie and Sacramental Ontology: A Return to Mystery*. Oxford: Oxford University Press, 2009.

———. "Redemptive Hospitality in Irenaeus: A Model for Ecumenicity in a Violent World." *ProEccl* 11 (2002): 207-26.

———. "Sacramental Interpretation: On the Need for Theological Grounding of Narratival History." In *Exile: A Conversation with N. T. Wright*, edited by James M. Scott, 255-72. Downers Grove, IL: IVP Academic, 2017.

———. *Scripture as Real Presence: Sacramental Exegesis in the Early Church*. Grand Rapids, MI: Baker Academic, 2017.

———. "Christopher Seitz and the Priority of the Christ Event." *ProEccl* 29 (2020): 275-84.

Briggman, Anthony. "Revisiting Irenaeus' Philosophical Acumen." *VC* 65 (2011): 115-24.

Briggs, Richard. *The Virtuous Reader: Old Testament Narrative and Interpretive Virtue*. Grand Rapids, MI: Baker Academic, 2010.

Brown, David. *Discipleship and Imagination: Christian Tradition and Truth*. Oxford: Oxford University Press, 2000.

Brown, Francis, S. R. Driver, and Charles A. Briggs. *Hebrew and English Lexicon.* Peabody, MA: Hendrickson, 1996.

Brown, Raymond E. *The Sensus Plenior of Sacred Scripture.* Baltimore, MD: St. Mary's University Press, 1955.

Carson, D. A. "Theological Interpretation of Scripture: Yes, But. . . ." In *Theological Commentary: Evangelical Perspectives*, edited by R. Michael Allen, 187-207. London: T&T Clark, 2011.

Carter, Craig A. *Interpreting Scripture with the Great Tradition: Recovering the Genius of Premodern Exegesis.* Grand Rapids, MI: Baker Academic, 2018.

Cavanaugh, William T. *Torture and Eucharist: Theology, Politics, and the Body of Christ.* Oxford: Blackwell, 1998.

Childs, Brevard S. *The Book of Exodus: A Critical, Theological Commentary.* Philadelphia: Westminster, 1979.

———. *Introduction to the Old Testament as Scripture.* Philadelphia: Fortress, 1979.

———. *Isaiah: A Commentary.* Louisville, KY: Westminster John Knox, 2001.

Congar, Yves. *The Meaning of Tradition.* Translated by A. N. Woodrow. 1964. Reprint, San Francisco: Ignatius, 2004.

———. *Tradition and Traditions: The Biblical, Historical, and Theological Evidence for Catholic Teaching on Tradition.* San Diego, CA: Basilica, 1966.

Daniélou, Jean. *The Bible and the Liturgy.* Notre Dame, IN: University of Notre Dame Press, 1956.

———. *From Shadows to Reality: Studies in the Biblical Typology of the Fathers.* Translated by Wulstan Hibberd. London: Burns & Oates, 1960.

Descartes, René. "Second Meditation." In *Discourse on Method and the Meditations.* Translated and edited by F. E. Sutcliffe. Hammondsworth, UK: Penguin, 1968.

DiPuccio, William. *The Interior Sense of Scripture: The Sacred Hermeneutics of John W. Nevin.* Studies in American Biblical Hermeneutics 14. Macon, GA: Mercer University Press, 1998.

Drobner, Hubertus R. "Allegory." In *The Brill Dictionary of Gregory of Nyssa*, edited by Lucas Francisco Mateo-Seco and Giulio Maspero, translated by Seth Cherney, 21-26. VCSup 99. Leiden: Brill, 2010.

Dunn, James D. G. *The Epistles to the Colossians and to Philemon: A Commentary on the Greek Text.* Grand Rapids, MI: Eerdmans, 1996.

———. *The Theology of Paul the Apostle.* Grand Rapids, MI: Eerdmans, 1998.

Dupré, Louis. *Passage to Modernity: An Essay in the Hermeneutics of Nature and Culture.* New Haven, CT: Yale University Press, 1993.

Edwards, Mark J. "Origen." In *The Stanford Encyclopedia of Philosophy*, Summer 2018 ed., edited by Edward N. Zalta. https://plato.stanford.edu/archives/sum2018/entries/origen.

Elliott, Mark W. *Providence Perceived: Divine Action from a Human Point of View.* Berlin: de Gruyter, 2015.

Eusebius of Caesarea. *Ecclesiastical History: Books 1–5*. Translated and edited by Roy Joseph Deferrari. FC 19. Washington, DC: Catholic University of America Press, 1953.

Evans, C. Stephen. "Methodological Naturalism in Historical Biblical Scholarship." In *Jesus and the Restoration of Israel: A Critical Assessment of N. T. Wright's Jesus and the Victory of God*, edited by Carey C. Newman, 180-205. Downers Grove, IL: InterVarsity Press, 1999.

Fee, Gordon D., and Douglas Stuart. *How to Read the Bible for All Its Worth*. 4th ed. Grand Rapids, MI: Zondervan, 2014.

Fowl, Stephen E. "Virtue." In *DTIB*, 837-39.

Fowl, Stephen E., and L. Gregory Jones. *Reading in Communion: Scripture and Ethics in Christian Life*. Grand Rapids, MI: Eerdmans, 1991.

France, R. T. *Jesus and the Old Testament: His Application of Old Testament Passages to Himself and His Mission*. 1971. Reprint, Vancouver, BC: Regent College Publishing, 1998.

Frei, Hans W. *The Eclipse of Biblical Narrative: A Study in Eighteenth and Nineteenth Century Hermeneutics*. New Haven, CT: Yale University Press, 1974.

Gadamer, Hans-Georg. *Truth and Method*. Translated by Joel Weinsheimer and Donald G. Marshal. 2nd. ed. Reprint, London: Continuum, 2011.

Gerson, Lloyd P. *From Plato to Platonism*. Ithaca, NY: Cornell University Press, 2013.

Gillespie, Michael Allen. *The Theological Origins of Modernity*. Chicago: University of Chicago Press, 2008.

Goldingay, John. *Approaches to Old Testament Interpretation*. 1981. Reprint, Toronto: Clements, 1990.

Gorman, Michael. *Becoming the Gospel: Paul, Participation, and Mission*. Grand Rapids, MI: Eerdmans, 2015.

Graves, Michael. "The 'Pagan' Background of Patristic Exegetical Methods." In *Ancient Faith for the Church's Future*, edited by Mark Husbands and Jeffrey P. Greenman, 93-109. Downers Grove, IL: IVP Academic, 2008.

Gregory of Nyssa. *Concerning We Should Think of Saying That There Are Not Three Gods to Ablabius*. In *The Trinitarian Controversy*, translated and edited by William G. Rusch, 149-61. Philadelphia: Fortress, 1980.

———. *Homilies on Ecclesiastes: An English Version with Supporting Studies—Proceedings of the Seventh International Colloquium on Gregory of Nyssa (St Andrews, 5–10 September 1990)*. Edited by Stuart George Hall. Berlin: de Gruyter, 1993.

———. *Homilies on the Song of Songs*. Translated and edited by Richard A. Norris. Writings from the Greco-Roman World 13. Atlanta: Society of Biblical Literature, 2012.

———. *The Life of Moses*. Translated and edited by Abraham J. Malherbe and Everett Ferguson. Mahwah, NJ: Paulist Press, 1978.

————. *On Perfection.* In *Ascetical Works,* translated by Virginia Woods Callahan, 93-122. FC 58. Washington, DC: Catholic University Press of America, 1967.

————. *On What It Means to Call Oneself a Christian.* In *Ascetical Works.* Translated by Virginia Woods Callahan, 77-89. FC 58. Washington, DC: Catholic University Press of America, 1967.

Gregory the Great. *The Letters of Gregory the Great.* Translated and edited by John R. C. Martyn. 3 vols. MST 40. Toronto, ON: Pontifical Institute of Mediaeval Studies, 2004.

Guarino, Thomas G. *Foundations of Systematic Theology.* New York: T&T Clark, 2005.

Guigo II. *The Ladder of Monks: A Letter on the Contemplative Life and Twelve Meditations.* Translated and edited by James Walsh. Kalamazoo, MI: Cistercian Publications, 1982.

Gutiérrez, Gustavo. *A Theology of Liberation: History, Politics, and Salvation.* Translated and edited by Caridad Inda and John Eagleson. Rev. ed. Maryknoll, NY: Orbis, 1988.

Hall, Christopher A. *Learning Theology with the Church Fathers.* Downers Grove, IL: InterVarsity Press, 2002.

Hanson, R. P. C. *The Search for the Christian Doctrine of God: The Arian Controversy 318–381.* Edinburgh: T&T Clark, 1988.

Harrison, Carol. "'Not Words but Things': Harmonious Diversity in the Four Gospels." In *Augustine: Biblical Exegete,* edited by Frederick Van Fleteren and Joseph C. Schnaubelt, 157-74. New York: Lang, 2001.

Hays, Richard B. *The Faith of Jesus Christ: The Narrative Substructure of Galatians 3:11–4:11.* 2nd ed. Grand Rapids, MI: Eerdmans, 2002.

Humphrey, Edith M. *Scripture and Tradition: What the Bible Really Says.* Grand Rapids, MI: Baker Academic, 2013.

Irenaeus. *Against Heresies.* ANF 1.

————. *Fragments from the Lost Writings of Irenæus.* ANF 1.

————. *Proof of the Apostolic Preaching.* Translated and edited by Joseph P. Smith. ACW 16. New York: Paulist Press, 1952.

Jacobs, Alan. "Love." In *DTIB,* 465-67.

Jenson, Robert W. *Canon and Creed.* Louisville, KY: Westminster John Knox, 2010.

Jowett, Benjamin. "On the Interpretation of Scripture." In *The Interpretation of Scripture and Other Essays,* 1-76. New York: Dutton, 1907.

Kaiser, Walter C. *The Uses of the Old Testament in the New.* 1985. Reprint, Eugene, OR: Wipf & Stock, 2001.

Keesmaat, Sylvia C. and Brian J. Walsh. *Colossians Remixed: Subverting the Empire.* Downers Grove, IL: InterVarsity Press, 2004.

LaCugna, Catherine Mowry. *God for Us: The Trinity and Christian Life.* San Francisco: HarperSanFrancisco, 1991.

Lane, A. N. S. "Scripture, Tradition, and Church: An Historical Survey." *VE* 9 (1975): 37-55.

Lauber, David. *Jesus as Israel*. Vol. 1 of *The Gospel of Matthew Through New Eyes*. Monroe, LA: Athanasius Press, 2017.

———. "Yale School." In *DTIB*, 859-61.

Long, A. A., and D. N. Sedley. *The Hellenistic Philosophers*. Vol. 1 of *Translations of the Principal Sources with Philosophical Commentary*. Cambridge: Cambridge University Press, 1987.

Louth, Andrew. *Discerning the Mystery: An Essay on the Nature of Theology*. 1983. Reprint, Oxford: Clarendon, 2003.

———. "William of St Thierry and Cistercian Spirituality." *DR* 102 (1984): 262-70.

Lubac, Henri de. "Hellenistic Allegory and Christian Allegory." In *Theological Fragments*, translated by Rebecca Howell Balinski, 165-73. San Francisco: Ignatius, 1989.

———. *History and Spirit: The Understanding of Scripture According to Origen*. Translated by Anne Englund Nash with Juvenal Merriell. San Francisco: Ignatius, 2007.

———. *Medieval Exegesis: The Four Senses of Scripture*. Translated by Marc Sebanc and E. M. Macierowski. Grand Rapids, MI: Eerdmans, 1998, 2000.

MacIntyre, Alasdair. *After Virtue: A Study in Moral Theory*. 3rd ed. Notre Dame, IN: University of Notre Dame Press, 2007.

———. *Whose Justice? Which Rationality?* Notre Dame, IN: University of Notre Dame Press, 1988.

Martens, Peter W. *Origen and Scripture: The Contours of the Exegetical Life*. Oxford: Oxford University Press, 2012.

McDonald, Lee Martin. "Identifying Scripture and Canon in the Early Church: The Criteria Question." In *The Canon Debate*, edited by Lee Martin McDonald and James A. Sanders, 416-39. Peabody, MA: Hendrickson, 2002.

McGuckin, John Anthony. *The Transfiguration of Christ in Scripture and Tradition*. Lewiston, NY: Edwin Mellen, 1986.

McKnight, Scot, and Joseph B. Modica, eds. *Jesus Is Lord, Caesar Is Not: Evaluating Empire in New Testament Studies*. Downers Grove, IL: IVP Academic, 2013.

Moberly, R. W. L. "'Interpret the Bible Like Any Other Book?' Requiem for an Axiom." *JTI* 4 (2010): 91-110.

Moltmann, Jürgen. *The Trinity and the Kingdom*. 1981. Reprint, Minneapolis: Fortress, 1993.

Moo, Douglas J. "The Problem of *Sensus Plenior*." In *Hermeneutics, Authority, and Canon*, 2nd ed., edited by D. A. Carson and John D. Woodbridge, 175-211. Grand Rapids, MI: Baker, 1995.

Moore, Stephen D. *Empire and Apocalypse: Postcolonialism and the New Testament*. BMW 12. Sheffield, UK: Sheffield Phoenix Press, 2006.

O'Brien, Peter T. *Colossians–Philemon*. WBC 44. Waco, TX: Word, 1982.

O'Keefe, John J., and R. R. Reno. *Sanctified Vision: An Introduction to Early Christian Interpretation of the Bible*. Baltimore, MD: Johns Hopkins University Press, 2005.

Okholm, Dennis. *Learning Theology Through the Church's Worship: An Introduction to Christian Belief*. Grand Rapids, MI: Baker Academic, 2018.

Origen. *Contra Celsum*. Rev. ed. Translated and edited by Henry Chadwick. Cambridge: Cambridge University Press, 1980.

———. *Homilies on Genesis and Exodus*. Edited by Hermigild Dressler. Translated by Ronald E. Heine. FC 71. Washington, DC: Catholic University of America Press, 1982.

———. *Homilies on Joshua*. Edited by Cynthia White. Translated by Barbara J. Bruce. FC 105. Washington, DC: Catholic University of America Press, 2002.

———. *Homilies on Judges*. Edited by Thomas P. Halton. Translated by Elizabeth Ann Dively Lauro. FC 119. Washington, DC: Catholic University of America Press, 2010.

———. *On First Principles*. 2 vols. Translated and edited by John Behr. Oxford: Oxford University Press, 2017.

Ortlund, Gavin. *Theological Retrieval for Evangelicals: Why We Need Our Past to Have a Future*. Wheaton, IL: Crossway, 2019.

Osborn, Eric. *Irenaeus of Lyons*. Cambridge: Cambridge University Press, 2004.

Parry, Robin A. *The Biblical Cosmos: A Pilgrim's Guide to the Weird and Wonderful World of the Bible*. Eugene, OR: Cascade, 2014.

Pelikan, Jaroslav. *Credo: Historical and Theological Guide to Creeds and Confessions of Faith in the Christian Tradition*. New Haven, CT: Yale University Press, 2003.

Pentiuc, Eugen J. *The Old Testament in Eastern Orthodox Tradition*. New York: Oxford University Press, 2014.

Pfau, Thomas. *Minding the Modern: Human Agency, Intellectual Traditions, and Responsible Knowledge*. Notre Dame, IN: University of Notre Dame Press, 2013.

Ratzinger, Joseph Cardinal. *God's Word: Scripture—Tradition—Office*. Edited by P. Hünermann and T. Söding. Translated by H. Taylor. San Francisco: Ignatius, 2008.

Riches, Aaron. *Ecce Homo: On the Divine Unity of Christ*. Grand Rapids, MI: Eerdmans, 2016.

Rieger, Joerg. *Christ and Empire: From Paul to Postcolonial Times*. Minneapolis: Fortress, 2007.

Rodger, P. C., and L. Vischer, eds. "Scripture, Tradition and Traditions." In *The Fourth World Conference on Faith and Order: The Report from Montreal 1963*. Faith and Order Paper 42. London: SCM Press, 1964.

Sanders, E. P. *Paul and Palestinian Judaism: A Comparison of Patterns of Religion*. 40th anniversary ed. Reprint, Minneapolis: Fortress, 2017.

Sandys-Wunsch, John, and Laurence Eldredge. "J. P. Gabler and the Distinction Between Biblical and Dogmatic Theology: Translation, Commentary, and Discussion of His Originality." *SJT* 33 (1980): 133-58.

Schmemann, Alexander. *For the Life of the World: Sacraments and Orthodoxy*. SVSPCS 1. 1973. Reprint, Yonkers, NY: St. Vladimir's Seminary Press, 2018.

Seitz, Christopher. "Canonical Approach." In *DTIB*, 100-102.

———. *The Elder Testament: Canon, Theology, Trinity*. Waco, TX: Baylor University Press, 2018.

Sheridan, Mark. *Language for God in Patristic Tradition: Wrestling with Biblical Anthropomorphism*. Downers Grove, IL: IVP Academic, 2015.

Smith, Kay Higuera, Jayachitra Lalitha, and L. Daniel Hawk, eds. *Evangelical Postcolonial Conversations: Global Awakenings in Theology and Praxis*. Downers Grove, IL: IVP Academic, 2014.

Steinmetz, David C. "The Superiority of Pre-critical Exegesis." *Theology Today* 37 (1980): 27-38.

Sweeney, Douglas A. "Ratzinger on Scripture, Tradition, and Church: An Evangelical Assessment." In *Joseph Ratzinger and the Healing of the Reformation-Era Divisions*, edited by Emery de Gaál and Matthew Levering, 349-71. Steubenville, OH: Emmaus Academic, 2019.

Taylor, Charles. *A Secular Age*. Cambridge, MA: Belknap, 2007.

Thate, Michael J., Kevin J. Vanhoozer, and Constantine R. Campbell, eds. *"In Christ" in Paul: Explorations in Paul's Theology of Union and Participation*. Grand Rapids, MI: Eerdmans, 2018.

Toland, John. *Christianity not Mysterious: Or, A Treatise Shewing, That there is nothing in the Gospel Contrary to Reason, Nor Above it: And that no Christian Doctrine can be properly call'd a Mystery*. London: Sam Buckley, 1696.

Toom, Tarmo. "Was Augustine an Intentionalist? Authorial Intention in Augustine's Hermeneutics." *SP* 70 (2013): 185-93.

Torjesen, Karen Jo. *Hermeneutical Procedure and Theological Method in Origen's Exegesis*. PTS 28. Berlin: de Gruyter, 1986.

Treier, Daniel J. *Virtue and the Voice of God: Toward Theology as Wisdom*. Grand Rapids, MI: Eerdmans, 2006.

Tyson, Paul. *Returning to Reality: Christian Platonism for Our Times*. Kalos Series 2. Eugene, OR: Cascade, 2014.

Vanhoozer, Kevin J. *Biblical Authority After Babel: Retrieving the Solas in the Spirit of Mere Protestant Christianity*. Grand Rapids, MI: Brazos, 2016.

———, ed. *Dictionary for Theological Interpretation of the Bible*. Grand Rapids, MI: Baker, 2005.

Vessey, David. "Gadamer and the Fusions of Horizons." *IJPS* 17 (2009): 531-42.

Wainwright, Geoffrey. *Doxology: The Praise of God in Worship, Doctrine, and Life*. New York: Oxford University Press, 1980.

Webster, John B. *Holy Scripture: A Dogmatic Sketch*. Cambridge: Cambridge University Press, 2003.

Wilken, Robert Louis. "Interpreting Job Allegorically: The *Moralia* of Gregory the Great." *ProEccl* 10 (2001): 213-26.

———. *The Spirit of Early Christian Thought: Seeking the Face of God.* New Haven, CT: Yale University Press, 2003.

William of Saint Thierry. *The Mirror of Faith.* Translated by Thomas X. Davis. Cistercian Fathers 15. Kalamazoo, MI: Cistercian Publications, 1979.

———. *The Nature and Dignity of Love.* Translated by Thomas X. Davis. Kalamazoo, MI: Cistercian Publications, 1981.

Wright, N. T. *The Climax of the Covenant: Christ and the Law in Pauline Theology.* Minneapolis: Fortress, 1991.

———. *Paul: In Fresh Perspective.* Minneapolis: Fortress, 2009.

Wright, William M., and Francis Martin. *Encountering the Living God in Scripture: Theological and Philosophical Principles for Interpretation.* Grand Rapids, MI: Baker Academic, 2019.

Young, Frances M. *Biblical Exegesis and the Formation of Christian Culture.* 1997. Reprint, Peabody, MA: Hendrickson, 2002.

SCRIPTURE INDEX

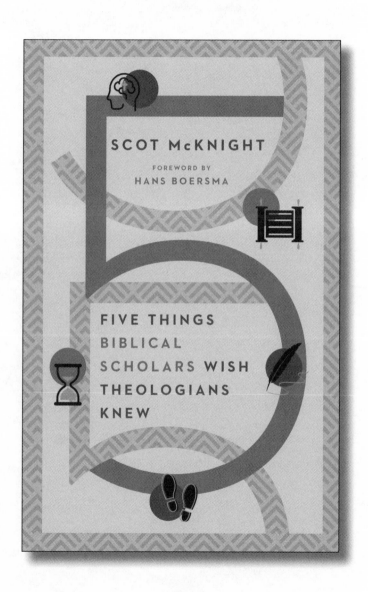

SCOT McKNIGHT

FOREWORD BY
HANS BOERSMA

FIVE THINGS
BIBLICAL
SCHOLARS WISH
THEOLOGIANS
KNEW